MW00908893

ONLY THE
TRUTH IS
FUNNY

ONLY THE TRUTH IS FUNNY

My Family and How I Survived It

RICK REYNOLDS

HYPERION

NEW YORK

Text copyright © 1992 Rick Reynolds

All rights reserved. No part of this book may be used or reproduced in any manner whatsoever without written permission of the Publisher. Printed in the United States of America. For information address Hyperion, 114 Fifth Avenue, New York, New York 10011

LIBRARY OF CONGRESS CATALOGING-IN-PUBLICATION DATA

Reynolds, Rick
Only the truth is funny : my family, and how I survived it / by Rick Reynolds.
p.   cm.
ISBN 1-56282-975-0 : $17.95
1. Problem families—United States—Humor   2. Reynolds, Rick.
3. Comedians—United States—Biography.   I. Title.
HV699.R395   1992
362.82′092—dc20
[B]

92-9643
CIP

FIRST EDITION
10 9 8 7 6 5 4 3 2 1

ONLY THE
TRUTH IS
FUNNY

SOULLESS ZOMBIES

My name is Rick Reynolds. I was born in Portland, Oregon, on December 13, 1951. As I write these words, I'm forty years old. I stand six feet two and one-half inches tall. I weigh 195 pounds. I have big hands, a big nose; I believe my penis to be of average size.

I'm losing my hair. Take a look at that cheesy picture of me on the cover. I wouldn't even have this pathetic wisp of hair on my head if I hadn't paid thousands of dollars years ago for hair transplants. I guess you could say I'm vain. I know that I care way too much what people think about me.

I'm insecure and often jealous of my peers. In fact, I sometimes hope for horrible things to happen to my friends.

I don't believe in God. I'm pretty sure that God does

not exist, although I hope he doesn't hold that against me.

I'm a very romantic person. I've been married for eight years, and I love my wife, Lisa Ludwigsen, more than words can say—even though the bitch wouldn't take my last name.

I collect old records, which I bring up only because I have so many (over fifty thousand at last count). I'm obsessive. It's a good thing I don't have any really bad habits. I don't smoke. I've never been drunk. I don't do drugs. Sugar, I do. I have almost no self-control with sweets. I can't understand people who do.

You know those people who can keep a big bowl of M&Ms on their coffee table as though they were a decoration? Days, weeks go by, and the M&Ms remain untouched. What kind of soulless zombies are those people? They're the same ones who will carve out a tiny sliver of fudge, nibble it, and say, "Oh, this is *so* rich!" I'll chisel out a four-inch-square slab and sit in the corner with my eyes rolled back, moaning, as every biteful explodes in my mouth like a chocolate orgasm.

I love for things to be in order. That's why I make lists. I have lists of everything: my hundred favorite records, my fifty favorite movies, my top twenty friends.

I've been putting together my Top Twenty Friends List for about ten years now. What I do is sit down toward the end of every year and figure out who my best friends are, in order of how much I like them. Believe me, this is much harder than it sounds. Comparing longtime friends that I have not seen for many years with newer acquaintances that I hang out with all the time is very difficult.

After the list is put together, I invite everybody on it to our annual New Year's Eve party. We eat, dance, and ring in the new year. About five minutes after midnight, everybody gathers around for the real reason we're there: the official reading of the List. I always start with number twenty, a person I like very much, but just not quite as much as number nineteen, and slowly work my way up to number one, my Best Friend of the Year. I also mention how they were ranked the year before, so they can watch their progress.

You wouldn't believe how much my friends get into this thing. One year a fight actually broke out between Tim and Jim (friends number four and five at the time) over which of them I really liked best. Another year, one of my wife's friends started crying when her name wasn't read.

I guess I have a lot of problems, so many that I don't have time to go into them all in detail. Suffice it to say I'm anal, obsessive, vain, quick to temper, overly introspective, lazy, judgmental, insecure, and self-righteous. Probably the most annoying thing about me is that I'm hugely opinionated. But I kind of make up for that by always being right.

Pardon me for noticing, but there are some good things about me, as well. For example, I'm the most honest person I've ever known. That might sound like bragging, but I believe it to be true. Besides, what's worse—thinking you're honest or saying you're honest? For some reason, in our society, we're not supposed to notice our good qualities. And if we do notice, we're certainly not allowed to mention them.

I am also the most open person I know. I have no secrets. None. I'm not saying that I have no lurid fantasies, embarrassing faults, or painful memories. Of course I do. But you know what? They become so much less lurid, embarrassing, and painful the more I talk about them.

That's why I wrote this book.

2

THE ROAD MOST TRAVELED

Basically, I'm a very simple person. Nothing brings me more pleasure than following my animal instincts. I love sex, for example. I know you love sex, too, but trust me—I love it more. I especially love those moments during sex when I stop being rational and I become a thrusting beast. I also enjoy my emotions, even the negative ones, because when I'm feeling them strongly, I'm very much alive.

When I'm driving, for example, and somebody cuts me off without signalling, I sometimes lay on the horn and yell obscenities until my brain kind of slithers to the front of my head. Suddenly I'm incredibly focused and "in the moment." I really enjoy that.

Of course, I prefer my positive emotions. I don't have to tell you that being in love is the best thing there is.

I would die for Lisa . . . I think. I mean, I can't be sure
what I'd do in an alley with some guy pointing a gun at
her head. I'd like to think I'd be noble, but how do I
know I wouldn't tiptoe off, stammering, "I'm not with
her."

I do know this, though: My favorite moment in life is
when I crawl into bed with Lisa at night. She usually
goes to bed a couple of hours before I do, so her butt is
hot by the time I get there. It's like a solar device that
stores up the sun's energy and emanates a pleasant heat
throughout the night. I scoot over next to her, into the
"S" position—that "spoon" thing—the front of my legs
against the back of her legs, my left hand on her right
breast, my weiner by her hot butt . . . and I'm just so
happy! That's how I want to die. I don't want to be in a
hospital with tubes up my nose. I want to be home in
bed, with Lisa in my arms, and just drift off. (I imagine
her waking up the next morning locked in that rigor
mortis death grip.)

After cuddling up, there's another huge animal bonus:
sleep. Don't you love to sleep? Actually, I can't be sure
I enjoy sleep, because whenever I'm asleep—I'm sleeping, for Christ's sake! I do know that I love falling asleep,
though, and I hate waking up, so that stuff in the middle
has got to be pretty darn good.

You know you're an adult, by the way, when you start
to love naps—middle of the day, TV on in the back-
ground, drool dripping into a pool on your pillow.

As good as sleeping is, eating is even better. Dinner
is almost always the high point of my day. I also love

eating junk food. One of life's little ironies is that everything that tastes good will either clog your heart or make
you fat. Incredibly delicious foods do both.

I remember my mother telling me I couldn't live on
candy and junk food. She was wrong. Sometimes I will
eat an entire apple pie—à la mode, no less—for dinner,
and function very well, thank you very much. I'll walk
and talk, speak and think, with nothing but apple pie
coursing through my veins.

One of my favorite moments in life is when I'm sitting
watching TV, eating a bag of Nacho Cheese Doritos (the
$2.69 big bag). I get about halfway through the bag and
I start to feel a little queasy, maybe a little guilty, because
basically I'm ingesting Orange Death. Then all of a sudden I have this glorious inspiration—I just say, "Fuck
it!" and finish the bag. I surrender to my Doritos!

I used to have a similar feeling in college when I'd put
off writing a term paper until the last minute. It would
be three in the morning and I'd be bone-tired, my mind
frazzled by guilt and lack of sleep. Suddenly a light would
go off in my head. I'd smile, lay down my pen, and
triumphantly announce, "I'm getting an incomplete!"

It feels so good to give up, to surrender, to take the
road most traveled. But it feels equally good to perse-
vere, to be strong, to work things out. In a way, we're
in a win-win situation in life. We can either glory in the
simplicity of that basic animalism, or we can seek higher
ground through rationality.

Philosophers have long referred to these two factions
of the human psyche as the "mind-body dichotomy." Part

of us wants to be an animal; part of us wants to be rational. According to conventional wisdom, the conflict between these two forces is the focal point of all human misery. I think that's wrong.

I see these two halves of the human psyche as somehow working together in a positive way. I mean, if you think about it, cows fulfill the same animalistic urges we do. They get hungry—they eat; they get tired—they sleep; but they are never actively "happy." When was the last time you drove by a big cow party, a field full of singing, dancing, merrymaking cows? The most a cow can ever be is content, because it doesn't have the mental tools to process pleasure.

I don't know about you, but I really like being rational. I love to think. I feel sorry for Lisa, because my favorite time of day—those twenty minutes between going to bed and falling asleep—does not exist for her. She falls asleep instantly. I don't know how many times I've climbed into bed with her and tried to have a conversation about a movie we've just seen.

"What do you think Spike was trying to say?" I'll ask, lying beside her in the S-position. "Can interracial relationships work, or not?"

"I'm not sure," she'll answer, seemingly full of energy. "It seems to me . . ." and suddenly she's out for the night. There's not even any warning—just "boom" and she's gone.

When I close my eyes at night, my brain becomes a slippery warehouse of ideas where anything is possible. That's when I ask myself the big questions in life—"Does

God exist?" "What is the meaning of life?" "Is there any fudge left downstairs?"

It's sad that there's so much more emphasis today on physical rather than mental pleasures. It's ironic, too, because I'm pretty sure that the more you exercise your brain, the more you come to appreciate the pleasures of your body.

I refuse to believe that ignorance is bliss. In fact, the smart people I know seem to enjoy life more than the stupid people I know. The smart people being my friends; the stupid people, of course, being my family.

If you weren't related to your family, would you ever see them again? Of course not. And I'm not saying the members of my family are bad people. It's just that we have nothing in common, and they're annoying. Every time we get together, all they want to do is dredge up the same tired memories over and over again. I don't think we've created a new family memory since the early seventies.

There's also a lot of historical revisionism going on in the family. Somehow over the years my Kafkaesque childhood has become, in their eyes, a Frank Capra movie.

3

THE SOVEREIGN LAND
OF CELEBRITY

It seems as though I have always wrestled with the idea of ending my life. . . .

What's the point? I don't fit in. It's not worth it. Why go on?

For years, I wallowed in self-pity over my brilliant insight into the meaninglessness of it all, and struggled to negotiate a precarious treaty between this empty life and its evil twin, death.

I loved to lie in bed and imagine my friends' reactions to the news of my suicide:

"He was a brilliant man," one would sob. "Life just won't be the same without him."

"I was afraid something like this might happen," another would chime in. "If only we had recognized his genius before it was too late."

An ex-flame would dab at the mascara running down her beautiful face and whimper, "Maybe I *should* have slept with him."

Sometimes it seemed to me that life was like a business that I was running in the red. The losses far outnumbered the gains. And though I'd toyed with the idea of closing up shop for good, I opted instead for longer and longer breaks—lying on my couch with a dozen donuts, wrapped in the numbing glow of my television. I think it's fair to say that for most of my life I've been out to lunch.

To make matters even worse, I believed that I had no control over my life. The notion of free will seemed nonsensical. I was born with certain instincts and hereditary traits, over which I had no control. An environment I had no part in choosing shaped my personality. At what point did I become "my own person"? At what point did I become responsible for my actions?

I felt like a pinball, pinging my way through life, racking up a score that was absolutely meaningless to me.

But I knew I would never kill myself, because I was afraid of death. Nonexistence is a little intimidating. It's also dispiriting to imagine life going on without you—and going on quite well, no doubt. If I left the world as the unknown schlub I'd entered it, nobody would remember me. I wouldn't have made my mark. I might as well not have existed.

I began to believe that the key to happiness was having a lot of people know who I was, so I became a comedian. For nine years people laughed at my jokes, applauded me on stage, and watched me on television. It didn't make me as happy as I thought it would, but I assumed it was leading me to where happiness was—the sovereign land of celebrity.

4

MAKE ME LAUGH,
MR. FUNNYMAN

I awoke from my dreams of fame one night in Dallas, Texas. I was headlining at the classiest club in town, The Improvisation. Apparently, it wasn't classy enough.

It was Friday night, second show. The moon was full and the crowd was ugly. I sat in the back of the room watching three hundred grown kids, full of booze and bravado, tear apart the master of ceremonies, a young local comic. Like sharks to blood, they were drawn to his fear. They taunted him with glee.

I was even more disheartened to see the second act do well. He was a mime and a juggler, which meant he would burn in hell twice, but that provided me little consolation as I watched the rowdy rabble leap to their feet to give him a staggering ovation.

I took the stage with a mixture of dread and anger. As any comedian can tell you, witty observations on life are

15

no match for a guy who can balance shit on his chin. As I began my forty-five minute set, it immediately became apparent that my regular act wasn't going to work. The room's attention span had virtually disappeared. I felt like a substitute teacher in study hall.

A few minutes into this nightmare a woman in the audience yelled, "You're not funny!"

I looked at her and hurled back one of my patented put-downs: "I thought only pretty women were stupid."

This got me my best laugh of the night, so far. A kid in the front row got a much bigger laugh, though, when he shouted, "Bring back the juggler!"

I began to feel my power as a performer slipping away. The audience was taking control. Out of desperation I dipped into that bottomless well of stock comic lines. "It's hard to believe that out of six billion sperms, you were the fastest," I shot back.

This prompted a huge laugh from the crowd. People were paying a little more attention to me now, so I launched into my "Big Butt" routine—my surefire, lowest-common-denominator material about, well, big butts.

But the die was cast. My two zingers had turned off the few reasonable members of the audience, and my obvious annoyance with them had fired up the others. People began to break into discussion groups, apparently debating whether to attack my personal appearance or my lack of talent.

Beads of sweat broke out on my forehead. I smiled, ignoring the din around me, and plowed my way through my act. The manager of the club, a short, harried man named Tony, was escorting a particularly obnoxious party to the door, when my microphone suddenly went dead. I looked behind me and saw someone hopping off the side of the stage. It was the kid who had demanded the juggler's return. Evidently, he had unplugged the mike cord. He returned to his seat, leaned back, and said, "Now make me laugh, Mr. Funnyman."

My memory of what happened next actually plays in my mind in slow motion. I could feel my anger well up, bursting behind my eyes in a red flash. Then, in a real sense, I went crazy. I jumped off the stage, grabbed the kid by his lapels, and pulled him out of his chair.

The room fell silent.

Tony, his mouth stuck in an idiot's gape, stood frozen. I lifted the terrified kid off his feet and threw him across the table, which crashed to the ground. With the sound of shattering glass still echoing in my ears, I turned to the stunned audience and said, "Fuck you."

As I walked through the crowd toward the front door, Tony followed me, frantically whispering, "Rick, what are you doing? You've got thirty minutes to go."

I ignored him and walked back to my condo, where I sat in the dark and tried to sort through the tangle of emotions running through me. I felt guilty, because I had let down the few people who had been on my side that night. I felt afraid, because I knew I wouldn't work for The Improvisation again, and they had provided me with a good share of my income. Mostly, though, I felt angry at the audience. As the anger subsided, I began to feel shame, because—as hard as it was to admit—I knew that I was wrong.

5

SOMEWHERE OVER NEVADA

As I flew home to Los Angeles the following Monday, I sat staring out the window and ran the scene over and over in my mind, trying somehow to justify my actions. The juggler (who, in all honesty, was a good performer and a nice guy) had finished out the week as the headliner. I was demoted to middle act. Everybody at the club acted as if they understood, even agreed with, what I had done, but I could tell that they all really thought I was crazy.

I noticed the woman seated next to me leaning forward, trying to look around me, out my window. As I leaned back to allow her a better view, I noticed, for the first time, that she was very pretty. She wore no makeup and had a fresh, open face. Her blouse was open slightly, and a satin camisole covered her breasts. Her chest was tanned and freckled. I guessed she was in her mid-thirties.

Watching her out of the corner of my eye, I was struck, as I often am, by the complexities of monogamy. Here was an extremely attractive woman, to whom I could not help but be drawn. But I was deeply in love with my wife. I knew I would never do anything to jeopardize that relationship. I suppose this is just another example of the never-ending battle between short-term pleasures and long-term goals.

I struck up a conversation with the woman over lunch and learned that she designed jewelry for a living and was on her way to a fashion show in L.A. I mentioned my wife several times during the conversation, hoping to keep the sexual tension between us at a minimum. As we talked, it became plain—at least to me—that we would have been close friends if we had gone to school or worked together. She had a simple charm that made me feel as though I had known her for years.

Somewhere over Nevada, she asked me what I did for a living. After hesitating, I did something I rarely do in life—I lied. I told her I was a writer, freelance, but remained vague about the details.

Eventually the conversation lagged and she drifted back to her magazine. I sat and brooded. After years of being proud of my career, I was suddenly ashamed of being a stand-up comedian. I used to love it when people asked me what I did for a living. Since I look like an insurance salesman from a bad fifties TV show, they were always surprised and fascinated to hear that I was a comic.

They would ask endless questions and weigh me down
with compliments:

"How can you get up in front of all those people every
night? You must be very brave."

"What's it like to bring so much happiness into people's
lives? I envy you."

"Have you ever met Sinbad? I think he's a genius."

Suddenly stand-up comedy seemed kind of dirty to
me—at least the way I had been doing it. I was sure that
this classy woman on the plane would have thought less
of me if she had known that I entertained drunken people
in smoky bars for a living.

I felt another one of my all-too-frequent depressions
coming on. There had to be some better way to make a
living. But the truth was, I loved comedy. I wondered
if there could be a better kind of comedy. Then I remembered something my crazy brother Mike had said
to me nearly thirty years before.

6

ONLY THE TRUTH
IS FUNNY

The hardest I've ever seen my brother laugh was at a newscaster in Portland, Oregon, who had a speech impediment. Why the guy became a newscaster, I don't know. He had a sibilant problem—he switched his "th's" and his "s's"—and I think the writers must have known that, because they gave him an awful lot of them in his stories. One night, for the life of this guy, he could not get through the weather report. Mike and I were howling. I think I was twelve years old, which would have made Mike fifteen, and we could not stop laughing. We literally begged for mercy.

"Please, please stop," we screamed, rolling on the floor in front of our old black-and-white TV set.

We looked back up at the screen and this silver-haired weatherman was staring right at us, sputtering, "Parthial clearing Sursay, the chanth of rain increathing sroughout the week." We laughed even harder. Three minutes must have gone by. Our lungs were sore. Tears were streaming.

Mike finally propped himself up on one arm, looked at me, and said, "You know, Ricky . . . only the truth is funny."

Wow. That seemed like the neatest thing anybody had ever said. "Only the truth is funny." I didn't know if it was true or not, but it sure sounded cool.

I wish I had remembered these words some twenty years later when I launched my career as a stand-up comedian. It might have cut nine frustrating years out of that career.

To be honest, I never enjoyed doing stand-up, even in the beginning. There was always an inherent deception in the delivery of my material that seemed almost sinister compared to the studied words of an actor. An actor gets up on stage every night and pretends to be somebody else. I got up on stage every night and pretended to be myself.

The main reason I didn't enjoy performing as a comedian was that nobody believed a word I had to say on stage. And for good reason—I lied a lot. I made stuff up every night so people would laugh. I don't do that anymore.

7

I NEVER WANTED
TO GROW UP

The most vivid memory I have of my childhood is of a sleepy summer day in 1966. I was lying on the lower bunk in our bedroom in Wood Village. The window was open, and I could hear a lawnmower way off in the distance. A warm breeze wafted in the window, carrying with it that rich smell of freshly cut grass.

I could hear my friends yelling up on Maple Street, their voices mixed together in a confused din. Mom was doing laundry—spin cycle—the faint scent of bleach in the air. I remember just lying there filled with this delicious sense of indecision.

I could go play with my friends, watch TV, or just lie there with my face in the sun and take a little nap. I could do anything, or I could do nothing. Hey, I was a kid!

That was really the best part of being a kid, which is why I could never understand why all of my friends were in such a hurry to grow up and take on responsibilities.

Would you have traded being ten years old for being eighteen, or being thirteen for being twenty-one? Not me. When does this desire to be older stop? You certainly wouldn't trade twenty-two for thirty, would you? When I was growing up, I never even wanted to pretend to be older than I was.

I thought it was creepy when my friends would swipe a cigarette or a beer, the icons of adulthood, and crawl behind the wheel of some old junker out behind Gil's Garage. They'd take a swig of beer and wash away ten years of their lives. Light up a smoke, slip her into gear, and go racing toward adulthood.

For what?

As awful as my childhood was, it still beat what the adults in my life had going. Adults had to work and pay for stuff and worry about everything. I never wanted to grow up. I still don't.

It's interesting that whenever I close my eyes and jump back to my childhood, I so often land on Christmas. I recall one Christmas morning, standing on the grate in our front room in Wood Village, heat soaking through my socks, rising up my bare legs, filling up my bathrobe like a terrycloth balloon. It was still dark outside and the lights from the tree were hypnotic. And standing there on my island of heat, breathing in the smell of pine and mentally unwrapping each present with sleepy eyes, I was filled with the kind of dreamy contentedness known only to children.

But Christmas couldn't hold a candle to summer. When I was a kid, June, July, and August stretched before me as an eternity.

I remember pushing my glasses up the bridge of my nose one sweltering summer afternoon as my brother and I dragged two large strips of cardboard up this huge hill in Wood Village we used to call "The Gateway to Heaven." The heat seemed to increase with every step, as though we were actually approaching the sun. My little sister, Candy, tagged along, frantically sucking her lower lip while keeping a close eye out for "gardener snakes." Our dog, Jingles, ran up ahead, occasionally turning to bark at us.

At the top of the hill we rested and tried to catch our breath. The ground had been baked hard, and everything around us looked dead, bleached white by the sun. The smell of dry grass hung thick in the air. Occasionally, Mike's hay fever would kick in, and he would let loose five or six violent sneezes that echoed in the sweltering valley below.

Mike, being the oldest, insisted on going first. He laid his piece of cardboard at the top of the trail, backed up to the barbed-wire fence, ran as fast as he could, dove onto the cardboard, and flew down the hill, holding on for dear life. I followed close behind. The exhilaration was incredible and, at top speed, a little scary. There was a large rock in the middle of the trail, so maneuvering was tricky. Even if you avoided the rock, there was a good chance you would end up in the thorn bushes at

the end of the trail. Bruised and scratched at the end of
the day, we still couldn't wait to come back for more
tomorrow.

Not all of my memories of summer are as wonderful
as those I have of cardboard-sliding with Mike and
Candy. I used to hate getting up at five-thirty in the
morning to pick berries. As soon as the alarm went off,
I began to devise excuses for not going. But they never
worked. I always ended up getting dressed and dragging
myself down to the bus stop on the corner. Sometimes
Mom would go with me. Before the sun had broken the
horizon, I'd be crawling through the dirt, my hands
searching through chilly, dew-soaked plants for straw-
berries.

We were paid fifty cents for each crate we picked. The
fastest picker in the whole field was my mom, who could
make up to twenty bucks in a six-hour day. I used to
make two or three bucks a day, depending on how much
I goofed off. I used the money to buy clothes for the
coming school year.

By noon, most of my last year's school clothes would
be strewn along the row behind me. In the oppressive
heat, the final two hours seemed to drag on forever.
Those days would have been intolerable had it not been
for my transistor radio. In the summer of 1967 I was in
love with a version of "Ding Dong the Witch Is Dead,"
by an obscure band called The Fifth Estate. I would wait
all day for one of the KISN Good Guys to play it. When
it finally came on, I was thrilled. But when it ended,
two minutes later, I was depressed, knowing it would be
hours before it would play again.

It is often said that smells bring back memories faster than anything else. For me, that would be true of music. Today, hearing an Elvis Presley song on the radio reminds me of buying my first Elvis album at a rummage sale in the Wood Village City Hall when I was eleven years old. I played it once on my brother's phonograph, and was hooked for life. I'm one of those die-hard Elvis fans. Not that I would ever make a pilgrimage to Graceland, or hang a black velvet painting of The King in my living room. I just like his voice.

Many of my fondest memories are of the most insignificant details of my life. For example, I have really strong memories of playing with the fat that hung from my grandmother's arms. I remember burning the trash on summer nights in the old burn barrel out in back of the house, watching the orange-edged ashes drift into darkness. I used to like emptying the wastebasket from our bathroom into the barrel. There was a lot of good flammable stuff in there.

Sometimes there were these big cotton things wrapped in toilet paper. I'd poke one with a stick and catch it on fire. Mom would lean out of the kitchen window and scream at me to "put that damned thing down!" as I ran around the yard with my little torch, an enraged villager, tracking down the Frankenstein monster.

There is no greater source of pain or pleasure for me than my memories, which allow me to make sense of my life, to figure out who I am by looking at where I came from.

8

LAST PIECE OF MEAT
IN THE WORLD

I have no memories prior to the age of seven. My brother claims to remember the day our real dad, Jack Reynolds, died. Mike was only three years old when it happened. I was only a few months old at the time, and Mom was still really a girl at twenty-one. Mom actually saw him drown. We were out on a picnic at the Sandy River, about two miles from where I grew up. Jack was swimming, got cramps, and went under. Mom tried to run out into the water in her street clothes and save him, but people held her back because the river was just too wild. She stood at the water's edge and watched her husband drown.

In one of Mom's old photo albums there is a picture of Jack kneeling in front of a '49 Ford. He looks to be in his early twenties in the picture, with his greasy black hair combed back into a ducktail. There is a tattoo of an anchor on his arm and he's smirking at the camera. I often stare at this frozen moment, trying to see something of myself in the face of this father I never knew. Of course, I never do. To be honest, I can see very little of my true self, today, when I stare at my own reflection in the mirror.

When I look at pictures of my mom in her early twenties, I'm always struck by how happy she looks—and how pretty, in her pedal pushers and horn-rimmed glasses. I always feel a deep sadness too, knowing that at that point in time her life could have gone a different way entirely.

Two years after Jack's death, Mom married my second dad, Len, an alcoholic who made our lives miserable for seven years. I don't have one positive memory of Len. In fact, I called Mom recently, and together we tried to think of one good thing about him.

All we could come up with was Candy, my sister, who was born in the summer of '58. I have a lot of great memories of Candy as a little girl. One of my favorites is of an incident at the dinner table when she was about six years old. She picked up a butter knife and held it over her head very dramatically, and said—this is a quote—"A knife is a knife, and a challenge to the death!"

Where in the hell did that come from? I've been watching old movies for twenty years, looking for that line. It's just not there.

Actually, knives were a big theme at suppertime in our house.

One night a particularly intense argument erupted at the table. Len stood up, trembling with rage, and kicking his chair out from behind him. Mom was scared, so she picked up her knife and threw it at him. It actually stuck in the wall, about an inch from his head.

I remember thinking, "Wow! Mom can throw knives at the dinner table! Jeeze, we're not even allowed to *sing* at the dinner table!"

That was an actual rule in our house, by the way: No singing at the dinner table. Lord knows what kind of anarchist I might have become without such parental guidance.

Another night I casually reached in front of Len for the salt, and he whacked the back of my hand with a steak knife.

"You know better than to reach in front of people!" he yelled.

He wouldn't let me leave the table, so I sat there bleeding and crying, and tried to finish my dinner. I put a yellow paper towel over my hand, and as it became soaked with blood, I began to feel trapped. Not just trapped at that table; I truly felt trapped in a bizarre childhood.

I remember one unusually humid summer night in 1958. Dusk was settling in over Wood Village, and all of the kids in the neighborhood were in our side yard playing our favorite game. Most kids had a version of this game. Basically, it had just one rule: Catch the guy with the ball and beat the shit out of him. The entire point of the game was to get the ball, which was ironic, because having the ball meant you would get the shit beaten out of you.

I know that some kids called this game "Kill the Guy with the Ball." In Wood Village we officially called it "Last Piece of Meat in the World."

Anyway, we were in the middle of a game this one night, and I remember chasing my brother's best friend, Warren Hagstrom, who happened to have the ball at the time, when I heard our screen door slam and a woman scream. I looked over, and in the glow of our porch light, saw my mom running barefoot across the front yard in her blue terrycloth bathrobe, crying. She couldn't move very fast because she was eight months pregnant with Candy. I watched in horror as Len caught up to her and tackled her right on the sidewalk. He called her a "fucking bitch" and dragged her by her hair back into the house. The door slammed behind them and silence filled the yard. My brother and I and all our friends just stood there, frozen. Nobody knew what to say. In fact, nobody has ever mentioned what happened that night. It is one of many similar nights that have disappeared from our family history.

9

READY OR NOT, HERE I COME

Although our house was small, we had a large side yard, which was the center of activity for the kids in our neighborhood. We played every conceivable game there. One of the more unusual games of the day was called "cigarette freeze-tag." In this game, the person chosen to be "it" had to "freeze" every other player by chasing them down and touching them. Once touched, you were "frozen" and could not move until you called out the name of a brand of cigarettes. No brand could be used more than once.

I suppose that if this game were played today, kids would call out the brand names of yogurt or, more appropriately, perhaps, the names of major carcinogens.

"Cigarettes!"

"Red Dye Number Nine!"

"Nacho Cheese Doritos!"

At night we used to play kickball, prison dodgeball, and Last Piece of Meat in the World until it got so dark we could no longer see the ball. We would stay outside until Mom called us into the house. The general rule was to ignore her until there was a slight note of anger in her voice—usually the third time she called.

For some reason, the mothers in our neighborhood always broke their children's names into two syllables when calling to them. I remember Mom standing on the porch yelling, "Caaaan—deeee! Riiiick—eeee! Myyyy—eeeek!"

After dark, our favorite game was hide-and-go-seek. One kid would cover his eyes and lean against the maple tree in the middle of the yard and count out loud to one hundred, while the rest of us scurried for cover. The kid who was "it" would yell, "Ready or not, here I come!" and we would all settle into our hiding places.

I remember trembling with excitement and terror as I crouched behind the burn barrel, waiting to be discovered. One night, the yard seemed alive with sounds, and I was sure that I heard someone approaching every few seconds. It was such a relief to finally hear someone yell, "Ally ally in-come-free!"

I guess I was afraid of the dark as a kid. For a while I had a recurring nightmare about my Grandpa Welter, my mom's father, who had recently passed away. In my dream, I would awaken to the sound of something tapping on the window next to my bed. I'd lean up and nervously lift one of the venetian blinds. Grandpa's face—his mouth twisted in a maniacal grin, his vacant eyes staring into mine—would be pressed against the pane. I always awoke screaming.

Mom's solution to this problem was to give me a night light. It didn't work. What is the purpose of a night light, anyway? It seems to me that all it does is cast an eerie glow throughout the room, so that on the off chance that there might actually be an ax murderer in your closet—lucky you, you've got a great view of him crossing the room to kill you!

I remember creeping down the dark stairway that led to our grandparents' basement with my brother. Each step down would reveal a different scent in the room: mildew—then laundry detergent—grease from Grandpa's old tools—and, finally, the acrid smell of the concrete floor itself. There was never enough light in the room, so the gigantic furnace, which held some ancient terror for my brother and me, loomed in darkness, its silvery arms stretching toward the ceiling. We would taunt each other to touch it, but each time we worked up the nerve to go near the monster, it would belch ominously and send us tearing up the stairs.

My sister Candy was terrified of our vacuum cleaner. It was one of those old Hoover uprights that lived in the closet. She would run screaming from the house whenever she saw it. I called it "Mr. Hoover" and drove her crazy by casually working it into our conversations.

"That's a pretty dress, Candy. Has Mr. Hoover seen it?"

One night, years after Mom had divorced Len, she

was out at the tavern and it was my turn to put Candy to bed. So at nine o'clock I took her little hand, walked her into her room and over to her bed. When she pulled down the covers . . . there was Mr. Hoover!

I was grounded for two weeks for that, but it was worth it.

10

OH YE OF MANY TALENTS

I got grounded a lot when I was a kid, a punishment I never really understood. I mean, can you imagine being annoyed with a kid and then forcing him to be in the house with you all day long?

Actually, "inverse grounding" makes more sense:

"Son, you're not allowed in the house or the yard for a month. Pack your bags and get out! I don't know where you're going to sleep, either. You should have thought of that before you sang at the goddamn table!"

You know what I think would be a good form of discipline? Let the child choose his own punishment. Have him go through the existential angst of making his own decision.

"Son, I think you know that you've been bad and that Daddy's going to have to punish you. So, I tell you what:

I'll let you choose how you want to be punished. I'll either spank your bare butt for one minute—it'll sting and you'll cry—or I'll hit you once, right in the head, and probably knock you unconscious. You decide."

It seems unfair that parents can punish their children however they choose. It seems even more unfair that they are allowed to make up any stupid rules they want.

"Kids, from now on when I come home, I want you to salute me," a father could order. "Every time I walk into the room, I want you to kneel and say, 'All hail, Sir Dad!' Come to think of it, I don't want to be called 'Dad' anymore—every kid calls their father Dad. From now on I want you to call me, 'Oh Ye of Many Talents.' "

I was once grounded an entire summer, for losing my glasses. I was throwing rocks down the ravine at the end of Elm Street with my best friend, Tommy Martin, when Tommy accidentally hooked my glasses with one of his fingers and flung them hundreds of feet, into the thicket below. We crawled down and searched for them for hours, but it was hopeless.

I remember standing in front of my mom, terrified, trying to explain what had happened. I kept glancing up at her blurred form, waiting for her to hit me; but for some reason, she didn't. She just said, "Go to your room; you're grounded." Two months later, I was still grounded, though I was allowed to play in the yard.

That summer I earned the money to buy my school clothes by selling almost everything I owned. Every morning about nine o'clock, I set up a small store in our front yard. I put most of my earthly possessions out on a table and sat in the shade of our poison-berry tree, and waited for customers. I sold records, models, go-cart parts, baseball cards, comic books—all of the stuff that crammed the drawers of the children of the sixties. I even hung balloons from the tree to draw attention to my wares. Ironically enough, this summer stands out more in my memory than any other of my childhood.

I always used to wonder why people have kids in the first place. When you think about it, what are children, really, but little stupid people who don't pay rent? And there was always something about babies I found creepy. Every time I held one, I had the sneaking suspicion that it would choke me to death for a cookie if it could. Face it, if babies were stronger than we were, we wouldn't think they were cute—we'd be frightened of them. What if babies started escaping from their cribs and gathering in packs? Imagine gangs of vicious, wild babies—black leather diapers, tattoos like "Born Yesterday" on their chests—spitting up on our lawns, gumming people to death, gang breast-feeding women. It's an ugly thought.

When it comes to children, I think there are two kinds of people in the world. (Of course, when you get right down to it, I think there are only two kinds of people in the world when it comes to just about anything. I love dichotomies. It's such an easy way to look at life—you're either this or that.) Anyway, with regard to children, here are the possibilities: You either have children, want to have children, love children, think children are the center of the universe . . . or not. I've always been in the "or not" camp, in part because kids don't get me.

As we were moving into our new house in Petaluma, California, a few years ago, a little red-headed boy from next door shyly walked up to me and said, "Hi. My name is Sean. I'm six years old."

I put down my box and stuck out a hand for him to shake. "Hi, I'm Rick," I said. "I'm six years old too."

Nothing. He just stood there staring at me as though I had sucked his little brain out of his head.

Children never laugh at my jokes. Lisa actually sat me down last year and told me that I was frightening the neighbor children.

I suppose she's right. If I had a six-year-old son, there's a good chance he'd live in a constant state of terror, because I'm unable to recognize that fine line between fun and fear. I can imagine tucking him into bed at night, giving him a little kiss, turning out his light, and then pausing for a few seconds in his doorway, silhouetted against the light in the hall.

"Wha . . . what is it, Daddy?"

"Oh, never mind," I'd coo sinisterly. "I just thought I heard something in your closet." Then I'd tiptoe out, plunging the room into darkness as I closed his door behind me.

Guess that's probably not such a good idea.

11

WRITER, COMIC, SUBVERSIVE

I like to think that I had a good sense of humor when I was a kid. I was always the class clown in school—the "wise guy" in my circle of friends. In fact, I'd say that I went through most of my adolescence with just two characteristics: loud and obnoxious. In other words, I was an asshole, which was okay, because it made me popular. I was extremely popular in high school, which is a curse in that it can make the rest of your life seem really boring.

When I went to college, I felt invisible. I retreated inward and studied philosophy, protesting my lot in life through my appearance. I let my curly brown hair hang down to my butt and grew a scraggly beard. I looked like Jesus on a really bad day. I took to wearing an Air Force jacket, replete with "wings," everywhere I went.

I thought I looked cool. Of course, looking at pictures of myself from those days, I know now that I looked like a moron.

I remember people staring at me back then, and even though they often looked at me with derision, I appreciated the attention.

I was picked up by the police once for hitchhiking, which was illegal at the time in Portland. While the officers were writing out my ticket, they ran my name and date of birth through their computer and discovered that there was a warrant out for my arrest. It seems that I had failed to pay an old jaywalking ticket. I was arrested, handcuffed, and thrown into the back of a squad car. On the way downtown I started berating the officers, in standard Reynolds fashion:

"This should be quite a feather in your caps," I taunted from the back seat. "Bringing in the notorious jaywalker, single-handed. Thanks to you, the streets of Portland are safe once more."

The officers were not amused.

At the station, I was photographed, fingerprinted, and told that my bail was set at sixty-eight dollars. I phoned a friend to bring the money and was put in a holding cell that smelled like a strange mixture of bodily fluids. After about ten nerveracking minutes in the cell, an officer came in and asked me to take off my jacket and hand it to him between the bars. Five minutes later he came back and told me that an additional charge had been filed against me—the illegal wearing of a military uniform, which was a federal offense. Bail was raised to over five hundred dollars.

About a week after my arrest, I was summoned by the
FBI to the federal building in Portland. I remember my
heart pounding as I rode the elevator up to the fifth
floor. The doors opened to reveal a huge picture of
J. Edgar Hoover hanging on the wall. Two agents walked
out, introduced themselves, and led me into a large con-
ference room where we sat at one end of a long wooden
table.

One of the agents brought out a small tape recorder
and asked if he could record our conversation. Suddenly
the cocky Rick vanished. I couldn't have felt more guilty
if I had committed murder.

They asked me a lot of questions about what I thought
of our country and the war in Vietnam. They wanted to
know if I belonged to any clubs or organizations of any
kind. I found myself answering all of their questions
honestly, without a trace of my usual sarcasm.

The lawyer who was later appointed to represent me
by the court screamed at me for ever having talked to
the "feds." He told me I'd be on their "blacklist" for the
rest of my life. It's weird to think that my name is in
some memory chip in some FBI computer somewhere
in the country, right now. "Rick Reynolds—writer,
comic, subversive."

The case ended up going to trial, but was thrown out
by the judge, who actually berated the prosecution for
wasting his time and taxpayers' money with such a frivolous case.

In some ways I could have been described as a hippie
in those days. But even though I looked like one, I cer-

tainly didn't act like one. I never protested anything. I never got stoned. I listened to The Monkees, for Christ's sake. Over the next six years I continued to study philosophy, and graduated from being a loud, obnoxious asshole to being a dark, brooding asshole.

12

MAN STAINS CARPET

What I liked about college at the time was that it put real life on hold. I was never very good at real life. Working, paying bills, getting married—all of that stuff was for grownups.

Even today, I can't believe that I'm forty years old. I remember when twenty-one seemed old, when thirty was ancient. Everything's relative, I guess. Today everybody seems younger than I am. I go to McDonald's, and there are fetuses working behind the counter.

When I was twenty-nine, back in 1981, I started to panic about what I was going to "be" in life. A lot of the people I had graduated from high school with had prestigious jobs; some owned their own businesses. I was a would-be writer, living in a tiny cubicle, making maybe five grand a year. I felt that I had gambled with life, and lost.

I had tried a lot of different jobs—a lot of different ways of "making it"—up until then. I was a disc jockey in the early seventies—the worst period of American popular music. You can play "Afternoon Delight" only so many times before being driven to the edge of despair. I sang in an ill-fated rock band, which finally broke up because we couldn't find a bass player we got along with.

Of course I went through my share of ordinary jobs as well. I filed bills for a hospital, worked as a messenger boy, parked cars, cleaned offices, washed dishes. Anything to fill in the cracks while I tried to write the great American novel.

Out of desperation, I entered a stand-up comedy competition sponsored by a radio station in Portland. It was held in a seedy bar on skid row, ironically named The Euphoria. I was nervous as hell when I took the stage that night, but somehow I managed to stumble through my ten minutes without making too much of a fool of myself. I ended up winning the thing, only because everybody else in it sucked just a little more than I did. When they announced that I was the winner—and you have to take my word on this—the place went crazy. I loved it. It changed my life.

It's kind of an old-fashioned notion, I guess, but I want to make my mark in the world; I want to stand out. Isn't that what everybody wants in a way? I know it's what the protagonist of every book I've ever read, or movie I've ever seen, has wanted—to be an individual. This is embarrassing to admit, but for some reason I've always thought that having a lot of people know who I am would help me accomplish this.

I want to be famous.

I know I don't want to be some unknown comedian when I die, which is what would happen if I died now. If somebody were to break into our house and stab me to death, the headline in the next day's newspaper would read, COMEDIAN FOUND IN POOL OF BLOOD. And I know it would be "comedian," because that's all you are in the eyes of the world—your occupation. You never see a headline like SNAPPY DRESSER FOUND IN POOL OF BLOOD. BED WETTER FOUND SLAIN will never appear in any newspaper.

The only exception to this rule is if you're famous. If most people in the country knew me—if I had done something substantial with my life—they would print RICK REYNOLDS FOUND IN POOL OF BLOOD.

I like that.

Of course, at this point in my career, they'd probably just print MAN STAINS CARPET.

In a way, I see my desire for fame as a bid for immortality. As I say, I fear death. As much as I've grappled with this concept, though, it's difficult for me to grasp the idea of my own death. Do you ever watch movies from the thirties and think, "Everybody in this movie is dead now?" Well, I watch movies from the sixties and think, "All of the dogs in this movie are dead now."

It's weird that we're all going to die, and I think that each of us tries in some way to reach beyond death. I know I do. I want to leave behind a body of work that somehow touches people when I'm gone. That's what I want from my life. Lisa basically wants the same thing.

She wants to have children, to imbue them with her sense of right and wrong, and to know that some essential ingredient of herself will pass from generation to generation.

A lot of people seek immortality through religion: Believe in God and your spirit will ascend into the heavens, where it will dwell for eternity. That's a beautiful program. I wish I could sign up, but I just can't make that leap of faith.

13

MIKE AND ME

I was eight years old when it first dawned on me that there was something weird about religion. I was sitting in the Wood Village Baptist Church one morning when my Sunday school teacher told us that Jesus turned water into wine.

I raised my hand and asked, "How?"

She smiled condescendingly and said, "Well, Ricky, it's a miracle. God can do anything, and you have to believe that to get into heaven."

But try as hard as I might, I couldn't believe it. I couldn't even believe that other people believed it. What I believed in at the time is what I believe in now: science. You show me a scientific principle that even comes close to explaining the changing of water into wine—some sort of "Chardonnization" process—and I might reconsider.

48

Besides, how good could the wine have been? It was thirty seconds old, for Christ's sake. Who would drink that crap?

Religion had another strike against it when I was a kid: my brother Mike. Mike has always been—and still is—the most annoying religious person I've ever known. He thinks homosexuality is a sickness. He believes that all Jews will burn in hell. He thinks women belong in the home. Mike's one of those people who has to talk to God, because nobody else can stand him.

When I was a child, it scared me that I questioned God's existence. I had a horrible fear of burning in hell for eternity. Mike once actually convinced me that I loved my comic book collection more than I loved God, thereby breaking one of the Ten Commandments. He told me I'd go to hell for sure unless I got rid of them. That night I fell asleep thinking of my hand on a red hot burner—holding it there as long as I could. I imagined the pain spreading up my arm, engulfing my entire body—and not just for a second or a minute or an hour of screaming agony, but forever!

The next morning Mike very generously bought all my comic books for fifty cents.

As awful as burning in hell for eternity sounds, there could be worse punishments, I guess. For example, you could burn in hell for eternity in a small room with my brother Mike.

One night, when I was eight years old, Mike announced at the dinner table that he was going to be baptized. Mom seemed pleased by the prospect, but—

even though we were Baptists—I had no idea what it meant to be baptized. So I turned to Mike's best friend, Warren Hagstrom, for some answers.

Big mistake.

Warren was the Eddie Haskel of our neighborhood, and even though he used to pound on me for the sheer pleasure of watching me cry and beg for mercy, I couldn't help but admire him. He was a rebel, swore all the time, and scorned authority. He could also spit better than anybody I've ever known. I once watched in awe as he jettisoned a wad of mucus into a soup can a good thirty feet away. I couldn't be sure he was aiming at the can, but of course he acted as though he was, and I was duly impressed. He wasn't a bad burper either, as I recall.

I used to covet Warren's model collection. He owned literally hundreds of cars, boats, and airplanes that he had painstakingly assembled and painted himself. They were on display in his room, which I was deemed worthy to visit only a very few times in my childhood.

When I asked Warren what "baptized" meant, he tried his hardest to convince me that it was when somebody was in such a hurry to get to heaven, they had their minister drown them. I spent the entire week believing that my brother was going to be drowned Wednesday night.

When the fatal night finally rolled around, we all got dressed in our Sunday best and drove up Walnut Street to watch Mike die. It seemed odd that everybody at the church was smiling and chatting with each other, as if there was nothing unusual about the evening's proceedings.

When the fateful moment arrived, I fidgeted in my pew, heart pounding, and watched Mike step into a pool of water. I know this sounds awful, but when our minister leaned him back toward the water, I couldn't help but think that I was about to get my comics back.

My first real brush with death came ten years later, when Warren was killed in a motorcycle accident. When I heard that he was dead, I felt no real sadness, only a kind of muted wonder. During the funeral—in which Mike was a pallbearer—I felt no sadness, either. Even after the reality of his death had sunk in, I remained unaffected by Warren's passing.

In the months that followed, I often wondered, lying in bed at night, if there was something wrong with me— if this lack of compassion for my friend meant that I was selfish or somehow coldhearted.

I never found an answer.

In some ways, I see this tragedy as a turning point in my brother's life. Mike seemed to grow up very quickly after Warren died—and he had made a much better kid than he did an adult.

Mike was always kind of eccentric. Every New Year's Eve he used to have all of us sign our names in a notebook. After we beat on our pots out on the front porch at midnight, he would look in his book and marvel at the fact that the signatures were "a year old." He also used to write notes to himself in this book that began, "Dear Mike of the future."

What's cute in a child can be frightening in an adult though. For example, Mike recently became interested

in handwriting analysis. Displeased with what his signature supposedly revealed of his character, he actually
tried to change the way he signed his name. He would
practice writing it over and over again, hoping to adopt
a new signature and, therefore—I suppose—a new personality. At least he was insightful enough to know he
needed one.

As a child, Mike also exhibited the kind of book-
wormish intelligence that looks nerdish later in life. In
high school, Mike was the classic nerd. He was a good
student, wore glasses, shunned girls, didn't go out for
sports, read a lot of science fiction, and was president of
the Chess Club. My teachers were very disappointed to
find that I wasn't the model student my brother Mike
had been.

Mike is a very intelligent person—always has been.
And he's a good guy. He would never hurt anybody.
There were times, as a kid, though, when he used to
take unfair advantage of his smaller and stupider brother.
He once gained "full control" of our bedroom by buying
out my holdings in the room. In going through some old
papers recently, I actually came across a clumsily written
contract that read, "Mike owns the closet and under the
bed." It had been signed, "Rick The Handsome Kid."

In adulthood, things came to a head between Mike
and me on Thanksgiving Day, 1989. It was a particularly
chilly afternoon, and we were all sitting around the dinner table, listening to Mike say grace as the fire crackled
in the fireplace. All heads were bowed, except for mine.
I was staring out the back window at some birds that

were perched on Mom's bird feeder. Mike kept glancing at me, annoyed by my spiritual indifference. I was off in my own world, thinking, "Do birds get cold? Do they talk to each other?"—just thinking my bird thoughts. When he finished the prayer, he surprised everybody by snapping at me.

"You know, Ricky, I'm really getting worried about you! I'm beginning to think that you might not go to heaven!"

I leaned toward him very calmly and said, "Mike, I don't want to go to heaven. You know why? You're gonna be there!"

14

TEEN JESUS

My brother is so exasperating. You must know the kind of person I'm talking about. Have you ever been awakened early in the morning by a Jehovah's Witness? Maybe you've been accosted by a crazy street preacher with a megaphone? You turn on your TV, and there's Tammy Bakker, Jerry Falwell, that Reverend Scott guy who never sleeps. Has it ever dawned on you that heaven might be a very annoying place?

Hare Krishnas have got to be the worst. You know why the Hare Krishnas preach nonviolence, don't you? It's because every time you see one, you want to smack him right in the head. I say, have at it. A good shot to the cranium might jump-start his sense of reality. Smack him a good one, and he might look at himself and ask, "What is this crap I'm wearing?"

One of my big fears in life is that I will have a son who, as a teenager, rebels against me by becoming devoutly religious. I can imagine pounding on his door at night.

"You're not praying in there are you, son?"

". . . No, Dad! I'm just masturbating!"

"All right, then. Good boy."

To be honest, there are a lot of things about religion that I like. In a way, I miss going to church, which is ironic, because I hated church when I was a kid. It's also ironic that the only time I remember praying as a child was lying in bed Sunday mornings, when I prayed that I wouldn't have to go to church that day.

Actually, if you believe in God, I envy you. You've got something I've looked for all my life and could never find—the answers to life. You know where you came from; you know where you're going; you know why you're here.

I think you're wrong, but I do envy you your conviction.

It's not that I don't have religious convictions of my own. I do. I studied religion for years. I've read the Bible, and I think it's the most important book ever written. That doesn't mean I'm about to take any of it literally. Like any document written by human hands, it has major flaws. Whoever wrote the New Testament, for example, didn't know a thing about character development. Just look at the treatment of its protagonist, Jesus Christ.

Christ first appears in the book as a baby in a manger.

The next time we see him, he's a grown man delivering sermons. What happened to Teen Jesus? I suspect they avoided this part of his life because he was a problem kid. He had to be a little spoiled. Imagine being thirteen years old and showing up at the father-son picnic . . . with God. You'd win every event you entered. Nobody can eat more pie than *God!*

I'm attracted to Eastern religions and Judaism because they emphasize self-improvement over heavenly rewards. I'm also fascinated by Catholicism because of all the antiquated doctrine still on the books, like exorcism. And trust me, exorcism is one of the least weird things about the Catholic church. The deeper you dig, the weirder it gets.

My favorite thing about Catholicism is confession. What a great idea. I wish there was a place in the secular world where you could go when you've done something wrong and have somebody in authority forgive you. Of course, penance would have to be a little different there—something like listening to five hours of National Public Radio or eating thirteen rice cakes.

I also like the Pope. Of course, everybody likes the Pope. Nobody ever says, "That fuckin' Pope! Pointy-headed bastard!"

Remember a few years back when somebody shot the Pope, and the Pope went right to the guy's cell to forgive him? That was cool. Of course, he is the Pope—what else could he do? He couldn't exactly sneak outside the guy's prison window and yell, "Missed me, missed me! Naanah, naanah, naanah!"

I saw the Pope when he came to the United States, a while back. I was disappointed, because you couldn't see him in the flesh. He drove by at forty miles per hour in that stupid Pope phone booth. Big deal. You know what might have impressed me though? Fill the booth with water, tie the Pope's hands behind his back, and give him a mile or so to get out of the thing. Let him show off his Pope stuff a little.

I used to have a bit about Catholicism in my night club act that always seemed to offend people. I'd say, "I might have joined the Catholic church if it was just a little different. If at Communion the Host was fudge, I'd be there for that."

When I added, "Body of Christ, with or without nuts," people actually got up and walked out, which always shocked me, because "Body of Christ, with or without nuts" is my favorite joke. I think it's the funniest thing I've ever written. It's strange that some people not only don't find that joke funny, they're actually offended by it. I guess I'm always amazed when people aren't just like me. And they should be, because I'm right about most things.

Aren't you?

I AM YOU

Don't you feel self-righteous about what you believe? Take the most volatile issue we have in this country today, abortion. Wherever you stand on abortion, no doubt you feel absolutely certain you're right. But are you? Have you ever tried to step back and look at it objectively? It's really hard.

I try to step back from the abortion issue and keep in mind that there are two sides to everything. On one side, there are people who believe that a woman has the right to decide what happens to her own body. On the other side, there are brain-dead zealots. Who's to say who's right?

There is no issue today that gets me more angry than abortion. But as adamantly pro-choice as I am, I wouldn't realign world thought along my own narrow view, even if I could. Without differing opinions, life just wouldn't be interesting.

I was sitting at a stoplight in San Francisco recently when a large tour bus pulled up next to my little sports car. For some reason I started staring at one of the passengers on the bus. Believe me, I am the least mystical person you could ever meet, but, watching this guy, I suddenly had the feeling that I was looking at myself. I knew exactly what he was seeing and feeling and thinking.

Sometimes I get the feeling that we're all the same person—that if a screwdriver could be dipped down inside my brain to some tiny screw that was the essence of me, and turned just a billionth of an inch, I would be you.

Don't you feel inspired when you finish the last line of a good book? Do you ever accidentally bite the inside of your cheek, then play with it for a week with your tongue? Do you ever clip a toenail and watch it shoot across the room? Of course you do—you're me.

In some ways we are all the same person. We all like good movies, walking along the beach, the smell of baking bread. That's why it's so remarkable that we're all so different. Some of us believe in reincarnation. Some of us believe in Judaism. Some are atheists. It's that metaphysical part of us that for me holds the most interest.

It's been years since I studied philosophy, but I still love the chase. I love those late-night, pseudointellectual bullshit sessions. Whenever I get into one of these discussions, it seems as though I'm always asked the same question:

"So, Rick, you're an atheist, huh? Boy, that's weird; you seem like a good person. What about your code of ethics? If you don't believe in God, how do you know what right and wrong are? Do you just invent your own morality? Are you your own god?"

As a matter of fact, I think that morality actually means more if you don't believe in God. It seems to me that if your code of ethics is imposed from without—if you're told what to do and then rewarded for doing it, or punished for not doing it—the notion of being a good person is lost. You're not being a good person; you're being self-serving. But if your code of ethics comes from within—if your heart's voice tells you what to do, and your reward is simply doing it—to me, that's the essence of being good.

Nor do you need a burning bush or a voice on high to teach you how to act.

Thou shalt not kill.

Duhh!

How many people have to flip through the Bible, going, "Jeez, I want to screw my neighbor's wife—don't know if I should!"?

Of course, knowing what's right doesn't necessarily lead to doing what's right. A lot of people routinely act as though they are more important than anybody else on the planet. It's easy to understand how they came to that conclusion. Each of us resides within our own mind, processing the world through a unique set of experiences. It is nearly impossible to feel as though other people are as important as we are. Nevertheless, we have to act as if they are. It's called being moral.

That's actually why I get so angry with people. I believe they know what's right, yet I watch them do what's wrong. People who talk in movie theaters are a good example of this. I can't tell you how angry I get at the movies when I've repeatedly asked somebody to be quiet, and they just give me a dirty look and keep on talking. If I could look at the back of that person's head, blink, and have his head explode, I'd do it.

And what about littering? Isn't the idea of throwing trash out of your car window unthinkable? And not because there's a large fine against it—you just know that it's wrong. If the fine was only two bucks, would you say, "Two bucks? Chuck it! Who cares?" and toss the crap out your window anyway?

My anger over littering has nearly gotten me into trouble more than once. I remember driving home from a comedy club in Los Angeles one night, in a particularly bad mood. My set had not gone well that evening, and I was very tired. I stopped at a light behind a guy in a Jeep and sat waiting, bored, my mind unfettered by thought. Suddenly, the guy in front of me flicked a lit cigarette out of his window, igniting my anger. I put my car in park, jumped out, walked over to the offending cigarette, picked it up, and flicked it back inside his car. The guy looked at me as though I was crazy—and, in a way, I suppose I was. He actually drove through the red light to get away from me.

I don't think a monetary fine is enough for littering. I think there should be a law that whatever you litter gets shoved up your butt! I don't care if it's a two-liter Coke bottle, for Christ's sake. Cops should carry Vaseline at all time. Imagine a highway patrolman standing beside your car, pulling on a rubber glove as he chortles, "It came out of the vehicle; it's goin' back in."

Have you ever been driving down the street with somebody you really like and seen them litter? This happened to me last year. I was with my seventeenth best friend at the time. He casually threw a banana peel out my car window. I couldn't believe it. When I called him on it, he bullshit-rationalized. "It's biodegradable," he said.

Come on. When you think about it, every single thing on this planet is biodegradable, in some amount of time. You could even chuck a piece of plutonium out your car window, drive by a million years later, and it's gone!

Hell, the human body is extremely biodegradable. That doesn't mean we should have funeral services out along the highway. Picture the procession rolling along about sixty miles per hour, and pallbearers heaving the body out of the hearse. The widow would drive by, weeping, her nose pressed against the window. In a few months the corpse would be kind of flat and dry with a little tuft of hair sticking up. That's just not a proper memorial.

Of course, talking in movie theaters and littering pale compared to some of the truly vile ways people treat each other.

16

I DON'T WANT TO KNOW

I'm engaged in an ongoing argument with my friends over the prurient nature of what is deemed "newsworthy" in our society. Obviously, many tabloid papers and news-magazine television programs are slanted toward sensational, often titillating stories. I think that a closer look reveals that even our most respected newspapers and TV newscasts focus almost exclusively on man's inhumanity to man.

Good "news" is bad news. When things go right, nobody cares. When people are kind, it goes unnoticed. But when a man goes berserk and slashes the throats of thirteen people—or, better yet, coeds—hey, that's front page stuff. Maybe I'm just a tad skittish, but I don't want to read about how he raped them before cutting their throats. This act somehow *diminishes me* as a human being.

I'm not saying that we should be unaware that such things happen. I just don't need specifics. Besides, how does such information arm anybody for the real world? If the murderer is in my basement, give me a call. Otherwise, I don't want to know.

17

A BITTER PILL

The worst memories I have are of the men who have populated my mother's life, beginning with my step-father, Len. One terrifying night in the winter of 1959, I was lying in bed, hoping to fall asleep before the nightly fight erupted in the front room. The fights generally followed the same pattern: First my parents would start drinking, then their voices would slowly rise in anger. Eventually a bottle would shatter, then came the sound of fist against flesh, and, worst of all, Mom begging him not to leave. But this night was different. The voices were louder; the anger was more immediate—nearly electric. The ugly fight shifted abruptly from the front room, through the hallway, until they were right outside our bedroom door.

Mom was screaming, "Not the boys! Leave my boys alone!"

Mike and I lay in bed, petrified. Suddenly the door

flew open and Len stood there, holding my mom, who couldn't stop crying, and he yelled, "Your mother's a whore! Your mother's a whore!"

He shoved her down and stormed away. Mom slowly pushed our door shut and lay on the hallway floor, sobbing.

It now strikes me as sadly ironic that as horribly as Len treated my mom, when he finally left for good she missed him, and there was a void in her life that she eventually filled with alcohol. She drank for many years, hanging out in local taverns and bringing home a succession of men who turned out to be just as mean to her as Len had been. I could never understand how my mom, who I thought was so great, could have anything to do with these drunken derelicts. I don't know how many times I had to tell my friends, "Oh, he's just my uncle." Today I understand that Mom was lonely; she needed somebody. But as a kid, in the fifties and sixties, it was a bitter pill to swallow.

I think my brother was psychologically affected by the presence of these men in our home. Mike was older than I was, and I think he keenly felt the moral implications—which were stronger at the time—of Mom's sleeping with men she wasn't married to. I don't even want to think about how it might have affected my sister, because Candy slept in the same room as my mom.

All I can remember of Mom's boyfriends are the fights—pulling the covers over my head and whispering to myself, "Leave her alone, just go away and leave her alone."

One night I lay there listening to one of those guys scream at my mom while he went through the cupboards, breaking every one of her dishes. I could hear Mom crying out in the front room amid all this thunderous noise, and I started crying too, and cried all night. To me, at the age of ten, this was totally devastating. I knew we didn't own our car, and I knew we didn't own our house; at that moment it seemed to me that all that we owned in the world were those dishes, and they were gone.

All my mom ever wanted in life was happiness, and even as a kid I could see that she was looking for it in all the wrong places. I loved my mom, but it wasn't always easy. I was actually kind of afraid of her when I was little, because she used to have such violent tantrums.

One night I spilled my milk at the table. As soon as the glass slipped from my hand, my heart started to race, because I knew what was coming. Mom had just waxed that day, and when she saw the milk dripping onto her shining hardwood floor, she went crazy. I belted from my chair as she lunged for me. She chased me into my bedroom, where I curled up in a corner while she stood over me, kicking and cursing. She beat us for years, up until the time that she was diagnosed as manic-depressive and began receiving treatment. She's still on medication to keep her stable.

I used to be afraid that I would turn out like Mom, because I'd have these huge mood swings; it was obvious that I didn't know where to look for happiness either.

18

A SPINELESS GOOBER

All the people who know me well (and there are at least twenty of them) would attest to the fact that I have had a certain amount of success in my life because I met Lisa. If we hadn't met, I really don't know what would have happened to me.

At the risk of sounding Buscagliaesque, I have to say that I may not believe in God, but I do believe in love. I resist admitting that because it has a very "touchy-feely" ring to it. Trust me, I'm generally a dark, morose son of a bitch. But without romantic love my life never would have been worthwhile.

Actually, I think I've been in love four times. I say "I think" because there were a few times that came pretty darn close. It's sometimes hard to tell where liking ends off and loving begins.

First I'd say to a girl, "I like you." Then I'd move on to, "I like you very much." Eventually I'd get around to, "I really, really like you." The next step was tough— "I think I lu . . . lu . . . luuuu—ike you, still."

The first time I fell in love was with a girl who rode my bus; let's call her Janice. I was a freshman in college then, still living with my mom out in Fairview, on the outskirts of Portland. Every Monday, Wednesday, and Friday I took the 18-Troutdale home from Portland State University. I had the hugest crush on this girl who rode the same bus. Her disarming smile and flashing eyes made me ache to touch her.

She always sat on the opposite side of the bus from me, and we would flirt with each other outrageously. I could barely keep my eyes off of her. She'd look at something out the window on my side of the bus, following it with her eyes as the bus moved, until her gaze rested on me. I would look into her eyes with obvious desire, and, after a dizzying moment, she would look away, blushing. I would feel a giddy sort of sexual tension wash over me.

I was too much of a goober to just walk up and start talking to her. I always envied guys that could do that, just walk up to a woman in a public place, like a bar.

"Buy you a drink? No? Your loss, babe." And they could just walk away, unscathed. Every time a woman rejected me, I'd hobble home and nurse my wounded pride for weeks.

So I had to devise a more intricate way of meeting this beautiful girl on the bus. The first thing I needed to do was figure out her name. As luck would have it, she sat next to another girl who called her Janice all the time, so I shrewdly put two and two together.

Then one day I heard Janice say, "It's three weeks until Halloween, and the boys have already put pumpkins out on the poles in front of the house." She got off at her regular stop on Halsey Street and walked down 146th.

That night I borrowed my mom's old Volkswagen, drove up Halsey, turned left onto 146th, and started looking for "pumpkins on poles." I didn't really know what they'd look like, but I figured I'd know them when I saw them. Sure enough, there they were, at the end of the block, two plastic pumpkins perched on lightpoles on either side of a driveway. I slowed down and read the name on the mailbox out front, then raced home and looked for the name and address in the phone book.

It took me a couple of hours to work up the nerve to call. As I dialed the last number my heart was pounding. It rang twice and was answered by the meanest man in the universe.

"Hello?" he grumbled.

I cleared my throat. "Hi, is Janice there?"

"Yeah, just a minute."

I waited, heart pounding, mouth dry.

"Hello?" It was the voice of an angel.

"Hi, Janice. My name's Rick Reynolds. You don't really know me. Well, you kind of do. We ride the same bus home sometimes. I have kind of long hair, and I guess I sort of flirt with you a little bit . . . sometimes."

After a moment she said, "Yes?"

All that, and the ball was back in my court already.

Anyway, I told her about the pumpkins on the poles, which she thought was cute, and we made a date for that weekend to see *Butch Cassidy and the Sundance Kid*. When I picked her up that Saturday night she looked great, and it felt strange to see her sitting there in my mom's car, right next to me.

I felt very cocky at the theater, because I was with the prettiest girl there. I threw money around like a big shot—bought the large Jujubes, jumbo Coke, the works. Blew my whole wad.

I don't remember very much about the movie, though, because I was too busy holding in my gas, testing my breath—all of that first date crap. I was also preoccupied with working up the nerve to put my arm around her.

It's always been very difficult for me to put my arm around a woman on a first date. Every time I ever asked a woman out, I hoped to fall in love with her, kiss her, touch her breasts, have sex. But I was never sure if my date wanted the same thing. For all I knew, she was just looking for a fishin' buddy. At any rate, to put your arm around your date is to let her know that you do want to move into this romantic/sexual area. It's a very difficult move.

After an hour of berating myself for being a spineless goober, I finally inched my arm around Janice. She responded perfectly, edging closer to me and laying her head on my shoulder. Her hair smelled so wonderful that night, and I was bursting with pride, because she actually seemed to like me.

When Butch and Sundance jumped off the cliff and yelled, "Shiiiiiiiit!" Janice and I laughed together, and looked deeply into each other's eyes. That tender moment before the first kiss has got to be one of the greatest moments in life.

She felt totally submissive in my arms, and I knew for the first time in my life that I would make love to the person I was holding. The furthest I'd ever been with a girl up to this point was "second base"—feeling a bare breast, which I liked—but I wanted more. That night I got more. I didn't slide into home, but I did steal third.

We were in Mom's Volkswagen. It was mid-October, and the windows were all steamed up. Janice was in her bucket seat and I was sprawled across the emergency brake with my hand up her dress, kissing her neck. That was the horniest I'd ever been . . . with another person present, that is. Do you remember how horny you got before you ever had sex—rubbing against each other, kissing, fondling? I could barely crawl out of the car that night, my balls were so huge.

We had sex five nights later, in my Mom's bed. (Obviously, she wasn't home.) To tell you the truth, it wasn't that good . . . for me. Janice dug it, of course.

19

WHAT A WIENER!

I've had sex with twenty-three women in my life. Some of you are thinking that's quite a few. Others are thinking, "What a wiener!" Twenty-three, and I've had crabs twice—which is a pretty good crab-to-woman ratio, I think.

I first got crabs when I was twenty-one, from a woman I met at a party. I was, for a brief period (commonly referred to as "the seventies"), a slut. I slept around whenever I got the chance. Unfortunately, that wasn't that often, because I was shy with women. This particular night I hoped to get the chance with an attractive brunette I found myself sitting next to on my friend Kevin's couch.

We started talking and flirting, and it turned out that she had heard that I was a notorious teetotaler. Apparently this constituted a tremendous challenge to her. She thought it would be fun to get me drunk, and proceeded to bring me glass after glass of 7Up spiked with vodka, which she insisted was straight soda. I played along, pretending to consume the drinks with gusto. When she would turn to talk to a friend, I poured the odious concoction into the large potted plant next to me. As I began to act more and more intoxicated, making sexual overtures well beyond my normal character, I figured out one reason people drink: It gives them an excuse. That night I was overbearing, but it was okay, because I was "drunk." It was especially okay because I got laid.

A week later I woke up in the middle of the night, itching to death. I went into the bathroom and picked a mysterious object off of one of my pubic hairs. Close up, it looked just like a tiny little crab. But I knew I couldn't have crabs, because only scummy people got crabs. Then the thing started crawling across my finger. That's when I first realized that I was scum.

One of the most embarrassing moments of my life was when I went to the free clinic the next morning and whispered to the receptionist that I had crabs. In front of an entire waiting room full of people, she yelled, "Crabs, huh? Must itch like hell!" My face turned red as the whole place burst out laughing.

20

THE MOST EMBARRASSING CHAPTER

The second time I fell in love, I got married. The way I treated my first wife is the most embarrassing chapter of my life.

I met her in college. To me, she was the embodiment of the perfect woman—cute, sweet, and intelligent, plus she laughed at my jokes. Her parents hated me from the first moment they met me. To them, I was the embodiment of the imperfect man—unkempt, overbearing, unemployed—and they never laughed at my jokes. Mostly, though, they didn't trust me. As it turned out, their distrust was well placed.

I don't like to talk about my first marriage. It's not easy to recount a story in which you are the villain. Also, referring to Lisa as my "second wife" seems to demean her—and our relationshp—somehow. And though I'm sure I learned a great deal from the mistakes I made, that knowledge certainly wasn't worth the pain I caused another person.

How I could have mistreated a woman I loved as much as I loved my first wife is still a mystery to me. Sure, I was depressed during these years; I felt unimportant; I feared the future. But that doesn't justify the way I bullied her. It doesn't explain why I was so stupidly jealous of her. It certainly doesn't relieve my guilt over the fact that I cheated on her.

I understand why my memories of the two years my first wife and I spent together are as sketchy as my memories of my early childhood: It's because I don't want to remember.

The fondest memory I do have of our time together is of the night we saw Elvis Presley. We were walking home from Safeway, loaded down with groceries, when two guys pulled up in a van and asked if we wanted tickets to see Elvis that night at the Coliseum. I laughed and said I'd love to see Elvis, but I could never afford it. The concert had been sold out for months, and tickets were being scalped for hundreds of dollars apiece.

They laughed and the driver handed me the tickets. "No charge, brother. Have a good time," he said, and they drove away. I stared after them in disbelief. According to the tickets, the show started at eight o'clock. I looked at my watch. It was ten minutes to nine.

We raced home and threw the groceries in the front door. We didn't have a car, so we ran out onto Broadway, where I stood in the middle of the street like a madman and waved down the first car that happened by. I told the middle-aged man behind the wheel that we had to get to the Coliseum as quickly as possible.

"It's an emergency," I pleaded. "We have to see Elvis."

He looked at us for a second, then said, "Hop in."

All we missed was the opening act. As we took our seats, the lights dimmed, flashbulbs began popping all around us, drums began to pound, and the hair on the back of my neck stood up. It was an absolutely incredible night.

We were divorced within a year.

Though divorce can be devastating—it certainly was in my case—I have come to realize that it's often a very good thing for the couple involved. There are many, many relationships that simply shouldn't be—where the partners argue constantly; where the only thing holding the relationship together is inertia. Inertia, I believe, is the primary motivating factor in all of life. You get started in a direction, and it's hard to stop. You get a summer job working at a shoe store and thirty years later you own a Kinney's Shoes. You meet a girl at school, have sex, fall in love, and thirty years later the two of you are muddling through life together, totally miserable.

Counseling can sometimes help this situation, but there is a remedy that's so much more effective—divorce. Divorce is like ripping a Band-Aid off a really hairy part of your body: If it has to be done, it's better to do it all at once than to pull out a hair a day for the rest of your life.

I feel uncomfortable coming out as a divorce advocate,

however, when I also believe that divorces should be
more difficult to obtain. After all, a wedding is one of
the most important events of your life. People fly in from
around the country, thousands of dollars are spent, a
sacred ritual is enacted. A divorce, on the other hand,
is generally conducted in some back room with nobody
present.

I think that there should be a divorce ceremony—paid
for by the husband's parents, by the way. That's only
fair. They would send out the invitations:

> *Mr. & Mrs. Jack Reynolds*
> *are embarrassed to announce*
> *the divorce of their idiot son, Rick,*
> *from that bitch, Lisa.*

The ceremony would take place at the same church as
your wedding. You'd have to walk backwards down the
aisle. The groom would take back the ring and give it to
the worst man. The bride would be accompanied by her
maids of dishonor, sluts in black. The more embarrassing,
the better. This is the breaking of a solemn pledge, after
all.

21

WHERE'S BOO-BOO BEAR?

I guess the one good thing about having made so many mistakes in my relationships over the years is that I have learned so much. I learned that every time I snapped at my partner, every time I was stupidly jealous, every time I hurt her feelings and didn't apologize, I formed a callus on her heart that would never come off. Eventually the pathway to that person's affection was blocked to me.

I was always intensely jealous with my girlfriends, especially with love number three, whom I'll call Patricia. My relationship with her was by far my rockiest. It began poorly—I "stole" her away from my best friend—and it ended, four years later, even worse.

I was sitting on Patricia's porch one night, around midnight, waiting for her to come home. We lived apart, but I generally spent the night at her place. I usually called before I went over, but we had had a fight the night before and I was anxious to make up. Generally, making up was so much fun that it made our fights worthwhile, but our latest fight had been a doozy, and I was worried that Boo-Boo Bear (my nickname for Patricia) was still mad at me. I kept watching the approaching headlights, disappointed every time a car swished by.

Finally, at about one in the morning, Patricia's old Volkswagen pulled into her driveway. I stood up and noticed that there was somebody in the car sitting next to her. It was a man. When Patricia saw me, she backed the car out of the driveway and drove away. I stood, numbed, as her taillights faded into the distance.

Three nights later she came over to my place to pick up her things. I had vowed to be strong and not break down in front of her, but I ended up on my knees, begging her not to leave me. What about our plans? What about the family picnics at her parents' house? I could change; I knew I could. No one could ever love her as much as I did. Tears were streaming down my face, as mucus bubbled from my nose. Needless to say, I looked good.

I couldn't believe that she didn't love me anymore. She was so cold and businesslike. All of our years together suddenly faded into nothingness. In a way I felt that I hardly knew her anymore.

I can still hear myself pleading desperately as she walked out the door, "Where's Boo-Boo Bear? Where's Boo-Boo Bear?"

22

DEAD TIME

A few months after Patricia left me, I won the comedy competition in Portland. I immediately sold everything I owned and moved to San Francisco, to make a new start. I met Lisa in a comedy club, where she was waitressing while studying communications at San Francisco State. The first thing I ever said to her was, "You are *so* cute."

Lisa and I had known each other only a few months when she had to leave for a monthlong vacation in Europe with her parents. I remember standing in her apartment in San Francisco, watching her pack. We were both upset because we were falling in love, and separating—even for a month—was going to be tough. Suddenly I saw her put what I thought was her diaphragm in her suitcase. When she left the room I could not resist the temptation to confirm my suspicion. I peeked under a pair of blue jeans, and there it was—a makeup compact. I felt stupid and ashamed.

I used to have a real problem with jealousy, which seems so ridiculous to me now. The stupidest kind of jealousy is over your partner's past. What does it matter what he or she did before you met them? That's none of your business.

I know, for example, that Lisa had sex before she met me. I can handle that.

Of course, she didn't *enjoy* it.

Lisa and I have had our share of problems over the past nine years. During these stormy times, Lisa has been the anchor that has held our relationship steady. As time goes by, we seem to get along better and better, which is good, because I've discovered that I can't get anything done when things aren't right between us. I brood and pace; I'm irritable and scattered. For me, the time between words of anger and words of love is dead time.

I remember one night, about five years ago in L.A., I got extremely mad at Lisa. Like most things in life, I can only tell you about this fight from my point of view. It began with me, the loving husband, lying in bed, minding my own business. Out of nowhere, Lisa actually had the nerve to tell me that she would rather have me go blind than have her brother die.

Well, maybe it was a stupid question. I just thought I needed to know at the time.

Some people give up on their relationships way too easily. They have a few arguments, and they're ready to call it quits. They don't seem to realize that love is like a windfall tax: It's a problem you should be so lucky to have. I don't care how much you love somebody, if you live in the same confined space with them, you can't help but get . . . well, *annoyed* from time to time.

How quickly love can turn to anger when somebody uses the last of the toilet paper without replacing the roll!

The last time I got really angry at Lisa was in New York City. I was performing Off-Broadway, and we were staying in an apartment on the Upper West Side. Our friends Andrew and Luchie, who live in the Village, invited us over one afternoon for lunch. We were going to take a cab, but they said that would be too expensive.

"Just hop on the subway," Andrew said over the phone. "Go down to the Columbus Circle Station and take the downtown D train. The stop after West Fourth is Lafayette. Get off there and walk up Broadway to Mulberry Street." He gave me his address, and I said that we'd be there in an hour.

Lisa and I left the apartment totally in love and extremely happy.

A few minutes later we were at Columbus Circle, but we couldn't see a subway sign anywhere. There were some stairs leading underground, though, with the smell of urine wafting up from them, so we figured it was worth a shot. Five minutes later we stepped aboard the downtown D train. Everything was going perfectly. It looked as though we would actually get there early.

Ten minutes later, the train stopped at West Fourth. I leaned over to Lisa and said, "Next stop." But it was not to be. We sat, not moving, for a good five minutes.

People around us began to murmur. Eventually an announcement came over the loudspeaker. It was hard to make out, but it sounded something like, "The D train will regronth intren the shee grail!" Lisa and I looked at each other, perplexed, and people began scurrying off the train like roaches. Not everybody left the train, though, so it wasn't clear what we should do.

Lisa finally walked up to a guy a few seats in front of us, tapped on his shoulder, and said, "Excuse me. Could you tell me what that announcement was?"

He looked at her and said, "Sure. They said that the D train will regronth intren the shee grail."

Apparently you need some sort of New York dictionary to decipher these things.

Anyway, this is where our argument started. Lisa wanted to get off the subway immediately and take a cab, just in case, but I had two dollars and thirty cents invested in this damned train, and I wasn't about to throw it away. I insisted we stay where we were. The doors finally closed, and we plummeted into the pits of hell. Lafayette was not the next stop, nor was it the next, or the next. We finally got off at Canal, and the conductor told us that the train had been rerouted. We were told to go around to the other side of the station, take the A train back to West Fourth, and wait for the next D.

Meanwhile, Lisa was becoming a burr in my ass. "Let's take a cab," she repeated over and over again, as we made our way to the other side of the station. "Let's take a cab; let's take a cab; let's take a cab."

For the next twenty minutes we watched a dozen trains

come and go, none of them ours. Finally, we gave up. As we emerged from the station I pointed out to Lisa that this was truly history in the making: I had been wrong twice in one day.

As soon as we were outside, Lisa resumed her annoying chant, "Let's take a cab; let's take a cab; let's take a cab." But I recognized the neighborhood we were in. I knew that Andrew and Luchie lived "somewhere in that direction," so we started walking. I was getting angry, because we were already late and Lisa wouldn't stop harping.

My anger nearly exploded when Lisa actually waved down a cab (without my permission!), got in, looked at me and said, "Are you coming?"

I struggled to control my temper and climbed into the cab. The driver took off, and I gave him the address. It turned out we were a block and a half away from where we were going.

Have you ever been in the middle of one of those really intense fights—you're absolutely livid—when it slowly starts to dawn on you that *you're* wrong? I hate that. And the weird thing is that you don't stop arguing. You've got too much "dickhead momentum" built up. I don't know how many times I've found myself on this downhill grade, unable to stop:

"Lisa, God damn it! I told you we needed half a dozen! Shit! Look at this," I'll scream. "You only bought *six!*"

At which point I have no choice but to stomp out of the room, going, "This house is a mess!"

23

MY HAIR GROWS IN ROWS

I'm glad I don't have to impress women any more. In the first place, I've never been what you would call "cool." It was always so much effort to try to appear cool on dates. These days, the only time I wish I looked cool is when I pass a group of young, hip, rock 'n' roll types. They look through me as if I'm a breeze passing by; or, even worse, they smirk at me like I'm their old high school principal. I'm tempted to walk up to punks like these and yell, "Look, I was slam dancing to the Dead Kennedys when you were in third grade, so back off!"

I'm also not a good-looking guy. It's not that I'm ugly. If I kissed you hard on the mouth you probably wouldn't vomit all over the place. I'm like most men—not bad looking. If I have an okay personality and I don't smell, you might go out with me.

I do think that I was robbed of my shot at good looks. See, when I was in the second grade I had to get these thick, dorky glasses. I wore the glasses until high school, when I got contacts, but I also got acne. I had horrible acne for years. As my acne began to go away, so did my hair. I never had one good year.

Today, most of my image problem has to do with my hair. When I started dating Lisa, I drove a little MG Midget convertible, and when the top was down my hair would blow all around, which made me self-conscious, because I thought she could see my hair transplants. The hair on top of my head grows in rows now, like a field of corn. In fact, I hate to say I'm losing my hair; I prefer to think of it as being picked clean by crows.

Not a day of my life goes by in which I am not bothered by my hair loss. I picture myself as a hip, good-looking artist type, but when I look in the mirror I see a straight, balding computer programmer. It doesn't feel good to look like a guy you would never want to hang out with.

I'd love to have thick, black hair and be really handsome. Then when I walked into a party, women would look over and think, "Who is *he*?"

In real life, when I walk into a party women look over, think, "Bald guy," and immediately resume their conversations.

It's one of life's little ironies that so many women are drawn to men who aren't going to make them happy. Say you're a woman out at a party—the rational half of you knows that in a relationship the balding, funny guy you're talking to would be good to you and would love you, devotedly, forever. On the other hand, the animal in you can't keep its eyes off the tough guy in the leather jacket with the thick, black hair and the cigarette dangling from his lips. You can tell he's not a nice person. You're pretty sure he'd end up hurting you. But he's still the one you want to go home with, because he's cool.

"I don't know what it is about him," I hear so many women say. "He's just so . . . cool."

Well, I think I know what it is about him: He's weak. He has to be, because nobody is really cool. Everybody is filled with insecurities and self-doubts. It's only the weakest among us who pretend to be immune to these human frailties, who pretend to be cool. I speak from experience.

Nobody ever started smoking because it tasted good. How many people take that first puff and say, "Mmmm, this is delicious!" People start smoking to be cool; it's the same with drinking. That's why kids start doing drugs—they think it's cool.

I wonder where these attitudes came from. How is it that smoking, of all things, came to be thought of as cool? Why don't women at parties say, "Check out that sexy guy in the corner—the one eating all the fudge"?

24

THE LAST COOKIE
ENJOYMENT

Lisa and I got married in 1983. My dream of being famous drew us immediately to Los Angeles. Lisa hated L.A. from the get-go, for all the reasons that make L.A. so universally behated. I must confess that I liked Los Angeles, and still do. What finally drove me from the place five years after we moved there was the entertainment industry.

Now, I don't want to say anything bad about the entertainment industry, but it does happen to be an ugly cancer that can consume you. It did me.

About three years into our stay in Los Angeles, my career was beginning to blossom. I was headlining around the country, doing national TV shows; I was actually developing something of a following. I used to hang out at the Improv every night, which was sort of the hub

of the comedy world in L.A. That's where I would get
together with my friends, most of whom were stand-up
comics like me.

Superficially, we'd talk about the things friends talk
about—"Hey, what's new? How's it going?" But that's
where any resemblance to real life ended, at least for
me. For some reason, I never thought to say, "You know
what? I'm really happy. I love a woman who loves me—
isn't that great? I have my health. I get to make people
burst out laughing for a living. What a great life."

Instead, what I would do when people asked me how
I was doing was brag. "I killed in Pasadena," I'd say,
jockeying for ego-position with whomever I was speaking
to. If necessary, I'd use hyperbole. A vague opportunity
to audition for the *Tonight* show would become "I'm
going to be on Carson." It was all about ego.

It was about this time that a really good (top ten) friend
of mine, Jake, got on the Letterman show before I did.
I was incredibly jealous, and I wanted him—my good
friend—to do badly. I watched the show, of course, and
I remember when Jake walked out onto the stage, I was
thinking, "He's going to bomb. He's going to bomb."
Well, he killed on that show, and when I went to bed
that night I was more depressed than I had been in ages.

There were other such incidents, but I think that one
more than any other really caused me to put my dreams
of grandeur into perspective. In the end, I had to ask
myself, "What kind of world is it that I live in, when my
friends' successes are somehow my failures?"

In 1988, I traded the old dreams for a beautiful old

Victorian house in Petaluma, where the sky is blue, the air is clean, and none of my neighbors has ever written a screenplay. It turned out to be the best decision of my life.

In the six years we had been together, we had never owned property. Once we had access to a little dirt, Lisa took to it like a gopher. I can't tell you how much my wife loves her garden, or how little this garden means to me. We'll be eating dinner, and Lisa will turn to me and say, "So, Ricky, how are those tomatoes?"

"They're great, honey," I'll reply. "You saved us a quarter. Thanks."

I never really understood the Zen of Lisa's garden until one night last year while I was watching TV. I love television, by the way. This whole anti-TV thing really bugs me. I hate it when I ask somebody if they saw a certain show and they smugly reply. "Oh, we don't own a television."

"Oh yeah?" I snap back. "Well, I have three, and they're on constantly!"

Anyway, about a year ago, I was sitting watching TV, eating a box of Mystic Mints, my favorite cookie in the world. Whenever I eat cookies I try to save the last one for special. But this one night when I went to reach for the last cookie, it was gone. To show you what a wretched husband I am, my first thought was that Lisa took it. Then I remembered that I had eaten the last cookie two commercials ago without even realizing it, so I never got that "last cookie enjoyment."

That's when I started to formulate my very simplistic,

very gooberistic philosophy of life: You should eat each cookie as if it is the last cookie.

Obviously, the last cookie's not really better than the other cookies. It just seems that way because you're paying more attention to it. I think that's the secret of life: You have to pay attention to the good things, or they're gone before you've had a chance to enjoy them. Otherwise, you're just another cow grazing through life.

As I sat there looking at my empty box of Mystic Mints, I thought again of Lisa's garden, and suddenly understood why it meant so much to her. What Lisa has done, in essence, is to take an insignificant thing, this tiny speck of earth, and make it significant in her life. I realized that I had always been unhappy largely because the details of my life were unimportant to me; I stood back from life and observed it.

The truth is, I'm never going to see the "tapestry of my life"; I'll only see the moments with which the tapestry is woven. The more I begin to live within those moments—the more attention I pay to the details of my life—the more I appreciate life.

Here's a perfect example of this principle: Those few extra minutes of sleep we sometimes give ourselves in the morning. The alarm will go off, and you'll immediately start calculating how much longer you can stay in bed and still get to work on time.

"I don't really need breakfast," you'll rationalize. "I ate breakfast yesterday; I'm feeling pretty good. I suppose I could wear my pajamas to work; no one would notice." Then you'll give your armpits a quick sniff and think, "I'll shower tomorrow. I just can't get up now!"

Those few toasty, luxurious minutes of additional sack time are worth more than an entire eight hours of sleep, because you're paying more attention to them. Do you know what I mean? Don't you just lay there in the morning thinking, "Ten more minutes! Oh God! I'm so happy! Don't look at the clock! Don't look at the clock!"

Then you sneak a look at the clock and think, "Okay . . . *nine* minutes—that's good! Nine more minutes!"

You can take those ten minutes and stretch them into an hour, just by paying more attention to them. That's basically what I did with summer when I was a kid. When I was little, everything in my life was new and interesting and riveting. Well, I'm not little any more. I'm buying a home. I'm married. I have sex all the time. Homework is not due tomorrow. As an adult, there are very few things in my life that rivet my attention on a day-to-day basis, unless I make them that way.

Sex is an exception, because it always forces me to be in the moment. It's the most riveting thing in life. Yet, even with something as compelling as sex, I can still lose concentration. I mean, I'll be doing it—it feels great— then all of a sudden I'll think, "Hey, Letterman's on in a couple of minutes."

25

BITCH, BITCH, BITCH

You have to take the time to consider the good things in your life, because the bad things hold more sway over you. Negative stimuli are more powerful than positive stimuli. Any experience can be ruined by one small detail.

I'll give you an example. Say you're out on a blind date, Friday night. (I'll do this from the guy's point of view.) You're at your favorite restaurant, and you can't believe that this beautiful woman is actually with you. She has the eyes of an angel, the face of a goddess, and the body of a two-bit hooker. As you talk to her, you discover that she's bright and witty (but not more witty than you, of course).

You drive her home, walk her to her door and she gives you a very soft, very sweet kiss—mouth a quarter-inch open, lips moist, eyes closed—perfect. You make a date for eight o'clock the next night and drive home half in love, half hornier than hell. The next day you can't wait for eight o'clock to roll around. You check your watch. Damn! It's only three o'clock! You take a shower, read a book, eat lunch, dress for the date, then look at your watch again—three-fifteen!

At a quarter to eight you're almost out the door when you get a call from a good friend you thought had died twenty years earlier. He explains what happened to him and you begin to go over old times, but still you keep glancing nervously at your watch. Finally you beg off, promising to call him the next day, and race over to your date's apartment so fast you get a speeding ticket, but even with that you're only a few minutes late.

She looks even better than she did the night before. You go to the movies, and after an hour of hesitation, you finally work up the nerve to put your arm around her. She lays her head softly on your shoulder and you become dizzy with the scent of her hair. That night she invites you up, and her apartment is incredible. She shows you her bedroom. You both sit down on her bed and start to talk. Then you put your hand on her shoulder and lean her back, kissing her hard, as your other hand makes its way slowly up her dress. You make love all night and drift off to sleep in each other's arms.

The next morning you awaken to breakfast in bed— eggs Benedict, fresh-squeezed orange juice, waffles. It's a beautiful Sunday, so you decide to drive out to the country. You lay down on a blanket and hold hands all day, just talking about life. The sky is blue, the air is heavy with the smell of pine, and you can hear the water of a nearby brook as it smooths the rocks on its way to the sea.

That night you fall in love in front of a roaring fire, your naked bodies entangled.

Yet, as you're drifting off to sleep, the one thing you can't get off your mind—the thing that sticks with you the most—is that damned speeding ticket. Because that's human nature.

I'll give you another example: Say you buy some rocky road ice cream that's incredibly good. There are hunks of fudge in it, marshmallows, nuts. It's delicious. Suppose you find one little thing in there you don't like— maybe a toenail down at the bottom. Suddenly you feel as though you've eaten a pint of frozen toejam.

Maybe you get a hangnail that you just can't stop playing with. Everything else in your life is perfect, but this one little hangnail becomes the center of your existence. It kind of hurts, but it kind of feels good. It's an in-between sensation. So you grab it with your other hand, pull, and it rips all the way up to your neck. You've got a long piece of skin dangling from your chin. I hate that.

Of course, some people live for negative stimuli. That's how they get off—by feeling sorry for themselves and complaining. They look for problems, and, naturally, they find them—everybody has problems.

When a complainer finds a problem, he always says the same thing: "I knew it!"

Go out for a walk with a complainer on a nice summer

day. As soon as he sees a cloud he says, "I knew it! Didn't I tell you this would happen? As soon as we left the house, I knew it would rain! I knew it!"

Ignoring him, you walk a few more blocks and it begins to mist very lightly.

"Oh, great," he sneers. "I knew this would happen. Why me? Why is it always me?"

You just start to turn back when a bolt of lightning shoots from the sky and hits him in the head.

"I knew it," he says, without missing a beat. "Look at this. My head's on fire!"

Bitch, bitch, bitch.

26

A MAGIC COIN

Suppose there's a magic coin that you can flip, and if it lands heads, you'll get everything in life you've ever wanted. You'll be incredibly attractive, rich beyond your wildest dreams, play the piano, whatever. But if it lands tails—you die. You instantly and painlessly pass from existence.

The question is, would you flip the coin and go for your fantasy life, or live out your normal little life in its normal little way?

I don't know if there's a right or wrong answer to that question, but I do know that it wasn't until I made the conscious decision to live out my normal little life, that my life became worth living.

27

A STRANGE MAN
SLEEPING ON OUR COUCH

I used to play this game in college where I'd turn off the pilot light on my stove, turn on the gas, then lay down on my bed, not allowing myself to get up until I could think of one good reason to go on living. (If I tried that today, I'd just say, "Fudge," and get up.) Well, one night back then I couldn't think of a reason. I fell asleep, and the next thing I knew, somebody had kicked open the door to my apartment, broken a couple of my windows, and was shaking me.

The first emotion I felt as I was coming out of it was embarrassment, because, well, a thing like this looks bad. The next thing I felt was fear—the fear I've had all of my life that I would turn out like my mom.

I remember, years earlier, walking up to my mom in the lobby of Gresham Hospital and asking if she was ready to go. She stared at me as if she didn't know who I was. The receptionist called me over, and I was led into an office around the corner, where I sat in an over-stuffed chair while a doctor told me about electroshock therapy: that it was painless, and that bits and pieces of my mother's memory would come back throughout the year. After these sessions I used to try really hard to convince Mom that she had borrowed money from me.

She never fell for it, though, because none of us had any money back then. We grew up poor, living on welfare and food stamps when Mom couldn't find work. I remember sitting on the kitchen floor going through all of the paper bags in our paper bag drawer, looking for change. The checkout clerks used to drop the change in the bags and sometimes a coin or two would get caught under one of the flaps at the bottom of the bag. I sometimes saved up my school milk money (twenty-five cents a week) and pretended to find it in one of the bags. It always made Mom so happy.

For me, the worst thing about being poor was that it was embarrassing. One day Mom sent me to the Wood Village Scotty store to buy some groceries. We were out of money and food stamps, so she told me to put it on our account. Al, the owner of the store, told me firmly that after that day we couldn't charge any more because our account was too high. I was humiliated because there were other customers in line who heard what he said. Two days later, though, Mom gave me another list of things we needed and told me to go to the store. I asked her for some money, and she again told me to charge it.

"But Al said we couldn't charge any more, remember?" I said.

But Mom wouldn't let something like that stand in her way. "Just wait till it's all rung up," she said, "and then tell him it's a charge."

"But . . ."

"Just do it!" she snapped.

I remember standing in front of the store for hours, trying to work up the nerve to go inside. I finally walked in, got the groceries, and stood in line. When I got to the checkout stand, Al rang everything up, then I said, "Put it on our bill, please."

Al was furious. "I told you your mother's account was over two hundred dollars!" he screamed, in front of the other customers. "You can't charge any more!"

"I'm sorry. I forgot to tell her," I lied.

"That's it! I don't want to see you or your brother in here again without money! Do you understand me?"

When I got home without the groceries, Mom yelled at me too.

I never resented my mother for the way she treated me though. In a way, I felt sorry for her, because she never seemed to be able to catch a break in life. Not until she met Don, that is.

I was twelve years old the first time I set eyes on Don. I was always the first one to get up in the morning at our house, and when I arose this one morning, I found a man sleeping on our couch. Of all the bizarre things I'd seen in my life up to this point, I'd never seen a strange man sleeping on our couch before. I got my

Raisin Bran and sat down to eat, and this mysterious man started talking to me. He was being really nice, which was weird, because Mom's boyfriends were never nice to anybody.

When Mike got up, Don was nice to him too. He was nice to Candy. And weirdest of all—he was nice to my mom. I'd never seen a man be nice to my mom before. They used to stand in the kitchen and kiss these long "movie kisses." If I had known tongues were involved, I would have barfed.

I soon started to see Don as our salvation—as my escape from this bizarre childhood, and Mom's long over-due chance for happiness. When they started sleeping together, I wasn't embarrassed or ashamed; I was happy. The happiest day of my childhood came a few months later when Mom and Don sat us down and told us they were getting married. I remember going into my room, with tears in my eyes, thinking, "We're going to be nor-mal now."

When Don got a job at the aluminum plant in Trout-dale, our lives turned around. He contracted to have a house built for us over in Fairview. I used to ride my Stingray bicycle over every day and walk through this big thing they were building for us. I got to choose the color they were going to paint my very own bedroom. I chose royal blue. My brother, Mike, chose glow green. When the day came to move in, it was like Christmas times ten. Now I could have my friends over without being embarrassed about how my house smelled. We lived in a nice neighborhood. I set my room up just perfect, with my black light and posters, my lava lamp, and all my records.

Don and I had grown pretty close by this time. I never called him "Dad," because I was too old, but I did learn to love him. One Saturday I was lying down in my room listening to our lawnmower go back and forth across our backyard. Suddenly the lawnmower died, and Don started screaming my name.

"Ricky! Ricky!"

I ran downstairs in a panic, and Mom and I ran out into the garage, where we found Don standing, holding a severed finger in his hand. We rushed him to the hospital, and they managed to sew the finger back on. It was a little short and crooked after that, but it worked fine. I was very proud, because even though everybody had been home that day, when Don needed help, he called out to me.

It was during this time that Mom really came into her own. She was finally happy. In fact, we were all really happy, until Don started robbing banks.

28

NINE PAINFUL YEARS

Don held up two savings and loans and a K Mart before he was caught. It turned out he was a compulsive gambler with a prison record that Mom didn't know about. He maxed out the Visa and MasterCard, wiped out the savings, and took out a second mortgage on the house. He left my mom with three kids and all these bills, and went off to prison for four years.

But Mom loved Don, and she stuck by him the whole time. She wrote him a long letter every day for four years, except every other Sunday when she actually drove up to McNeil Island Penitentiary in Washington to be with him.

I went up to the prison once myself. Don had been in about three years when he received his high school equivalency diploma, and they had a graduation cere-

104

mony for him. I don't know if there was a prom afterwards or not.

It's hard to believe, but every Christmas for four years Don sent me the same gift: a ski mask he had crocheted for me in prison. I swear to God! I don't know if this was a hint that he wanted me to follow in his footsteps or what.

The day he was paroled we tied yellow ribbons around the poison berry bushes out front to welcome him home. It was good to have him back. That night we played Uno until the sun came up, and our house was back in order. It was amazing how quickly we resumed the normal pace of our lives, as though Don had only been gone a few weeks.

One day, about a year and a half later, Mom was driving home from the Jantzen knitting mill, where she still works. She was listening to the radio, and they announced on the news that Donald Chase had been arrested for embezzling over twenty-five thousand dollars from his job with a government housing agency. During his trial it was revealed that he'd been gambling for over a year. He went back to prison and Mom divorced him. I never saw him again.

This was about the time I moved out of the house. Mike continued living with Mom for years, but I couldn't. Maybe I should have, but the house was just too stagnant and depressing after that. I had to leave.

Nine painful years went by without Mom's ever mentioning Don's name. Then one night she called me and I knew something was wrong right away. She told me that she had just heard from my sister, Candy, that Don had died of cancer in a halfway house in Portland.

Mom was crying when she told me.

29

A SICK SENSE OF HUMOR

My big fear in life had always been that I would turn out like my mom. Yet in recent years I have realized that most of my best qualities came from this woman. I know that's where I got my sense of humor.

We laughed a lot together when I was growing up. Mom's favorite celebrity has always been Bob Hope; she just loves the guy. One morning, when I was about ten, I was sitting with her at the breakfast table, looking at the paper. I held it up and pretended to read: BOB HOPE DEAD AT 63.

Mom's face turned white. "Oh no! What a shame!" she stammered.

I started to laugh really hard. She grabbed the paper from me, saw that I was lying, looked at me—trying to be mad—and burst out laughing. I still call Mom about twice a year just to tell her that Bob Hope is dead.

I also blame my mother for the depth of my emotions. You know you're too easily moved to tears when you bawl at long distance phone commercials.

I would give anything to die before Lisa. I don't think I have the emotional tools to cope with her death. When Magic Johnson announced he had the AIDS virus, I cried. When I see an elderly man in a restaurant eating by himself, I always get tears in my eyes. I imagine that his wife of many years has passed away. I picture him waking up in the morning, alone, and for a brief second thinking his wife is lying beside him. It is the saddest thing in the world to me. So I make a joke about him. I have what is commonly referred to as a "sick" sense of humor. For me, as for my mother, it's my defense against the pain of life.

I was walking through downtown San Francisco once with a friend, and we noticed a well-dressed man in front of us. He had a briefcase in one hand and a hook where the other hand should have been. I started making jokes.

"Hey, look at the guy with the hook," I said. "Who'd put a hook at the end of their arm?"

Obviously, I made sure he couldn't hear me. I would never hurt his feelings (or risk getting a hook in the side of the head). It's just that I felt really bad for him, so I made jokes to ease the pain.

How many times a day, after all, can you use a big hook? If I lost one of my hands, one of the last things I'd think to replace it with would be a big hook. A toilet plunger would come to mind before a big hook, or, better yet, I'd have the key to my house sticking out of my sleeve—at least I could use that a couple of times a day.

Make it detachable—now it's a flashlight; now it's a Dust-buster. I don't think I've ever said, "Honey, where's the big hook? Shoot, when you need the hook you can never find the damned thing!"

Big-hook jokes epitomize my sense of humor. I know they're not for everybody. It's like "Body of Christ, with or without nuts." They're potentially offensive, but damned funny.

Which brings me to my favorite dichotomy.

I actually got this from an article in the *Village Voice* in which the writer suggested that everyone in the world, without exception, is either a creep or an asshole. I think that's true. I'm an asshole; my wife's a creep. Do you know what you are?

If you're not sure, you're a creep, because assholes know they're assholes and they're proud of it.

Let me tell you a joke. The way you respond to it should reveal whether you're a creep or an asshole (that is, unless you've heard the joke before). I first heard it when I was ten years old:

There's a man pacing in a hospital waiting room, waiting for his wife to give birth (this is before Lamaze, obviously). They've already had a number of children, but they've all been horribly deformed. (Do you like it so far? Wait, it gets better . . .) Eventually, the doctor walks in, a look of consternation on his face.

"Mr. Smith, would you love your baby if it had no arms or legs?" he asks.

"Oh my God! Yes, I would. Just take me to my wife and child."

So the doctor leads him down this corridor, through

the hallway, into the delivery room. There he finds his wife in bed, a big bundle in her arms. He gingerly tiptoes over and peels back the blanket, revealing a giant ten-pound eyeball.

"Oh my God!" he screams. "What could be worse?"

The doctor looks at him and says, "He's blind."

Now, if you laughed at that joke, you're an asshole. Good for you—so am I. If you shook your head and said, "Hmmmm, no," you're a creep. Which is okay, too. This is not a value judgment. Lisa's a creep, and I love her very much. You were born a creep or an asshole, and you'll die a creep or an asshole. You can't change your creep/asshole status—it's a constant throughout your entire life.

Try going through your own top-twenty-friend list and seeing if you can conclusively determine who's a creep and who's an asshole. It's not always obvious.

30

FUNNY WASN'T ENOUGH

Believe it or not, my superreligious brother Mike is a huge asshole. He laughs at the sickest things in life—like newscasters with speech impediments, for example.

I sometimes wonder what would have happened with my career if I hadn't remembered that insignificant moment when my crazy brother turned to me nearly thirty years before and said, "Only the truth is funny." I could never have guessed that this one little sentence would completely change my life.

And though it was obvious to me that Mike's little insight wasn't literally true, while flying home from Dallas a few years ago I became intrigued with the idea of telling only the truth on stage. So I started pulling everything out of my act that wasn't factual. Which turned out to be just about everything.

I used to have a bit in my act about going out to a Chinese restaurant before the show with the other comics on the bill. I'd say that the fortune in the MC's fortune cookie that night read, "You will have good luck in love," and that he had actually just met a woman with whom he was falling in love. I'd tell the audience that the middle act's fortune was "You will take a long trip." I'd say that this was kind of weird, because he happened to be leaving at the end of the week for Alaska. My fortune that night, I'd claim, was "You make God sick." After explaining that it seemed to be my lot to always get the worst fortunes, I'd pull some more out of my pocket and pretend to read aloud: "A small child's testimony will land you in prison." "A psychic will lead the police to your body." And my personal favorite, "Jim Jones says 'Hi.' "

When I told other comics that I was going to drop this bit because it wasn't "the truth," they all said the same thing: "Who cares if it's the truth? It's funny, isn't it?"

That seemed really telling to me. Stand-up comedy had become "just something funny"—and no more. When your job is to cram twenty laughs into six minutes, you don't have time to make a point. You certainly don't have the luxury of trying to be real. Comedy today is instant gratification, the rock 'n' roll of the nineties. This makes me sad, because there was a time when comedy was jazz, and really hip people went to the Purple Onion to see Lenny Bruce be more than just funny. They stood in line outside the Hungry I to see Mort Sahl take his time. In New York they could go on Broadway to spend an evening with Mike Nichols and Elaine May.

After nine years of stand-up comedy, being funny wasn't enough for me any more. I had reached a point in my life where I felt that what I was doing for a living was frivolous. The only reason I went to work was to make money and to try to become famous.

So Lisa and I moved to Petaluma, where I started to piece together the puzzle of my life. I began to make some quantum leaps in my own personal happiness. I had chosen quality of life over fame, and I was beginning to live in the moment. I'd made the decision to try to do something meaningful in my work. I had many of what I would call the "ingredients of happiness." But, still, something was missing. I had a very Peggy Lee-esque sensation.

I looked at my life and asked, "Is that all there is?"

31

A CRYING, POOPING SHACKLE

Then one day Lisa called me from her doctor's office to tell me she was pregnant.

"Oh, honey, great news!" I purred into the phone. "Come on home! We'll celebrate!"

I hung up the phone and screamed.

We were going to have a baby: a crying, pooping shackle around our ankles for the rest of our lives. I didn't want the responsibility of a baby. I wasn't ready to be an adult. I had no idea how to parent; in fact, I'd had nothing but bad examples set for me my whole childhood. I didn't even like children, let alone feel capable of loving them. This did not seem like a good move.

As we got closer and closer to the blessed event, the whole thing seemed more and more unreal to me. Lisa was about six months along when I made the mistake of telling her I didn't need to be with her in the delivery room. Politically, a very bad move.

"I know it's the nineties thing to do," I admitted. "But let's try the fifties thing this one time."

She shot me one of those looks of death. I immediately said, "Kidding! Come on, honey, can't you tell when I'm joking?"

So, we started going to Lamaze class, which I hated with a deep passion. A friend of mine recently attended his Lamaze class reunion. Ughh! I never want to see those people again in my life. The thing that most bothered me about Lamaze class was that it was so damned precious, so sickeningly sweet. That first night, all of the men had to give a little speech about why they were there. I thought I was going to vomit.

"I'm here tonight to help my beautiful wife, Lisa, and to share in this glorious moment," I said, gagging.

The truth was that I didn't believe it was going to be a beautiful moment at all. I thought it would be like a car accident. Have you ever been in a serious car accident where you sort of floated above the reality of the moment? I thought it would be like that. I also thought that Lisa would be in a great deal of pain and that I'd be emotionally detached from the whole thing.

Well, on January 6, 1991, three weeks before Cooper was due, and way before we were ready for him, Lisa and I were sitting watching TV. Lisa got up and went into the bathroom, came back, and said, "There's water coming out of me."

I looked at her and said, ". . . Pee?"

I had always thought that when the water broke there would be a lot of it, but there was just a little trickle. It kept trickling for hours, so we ended up going into the hospital that day, Sunday. Cooper was born on Tuesday. There's a world of time between those two days. It was not the perfect birth we had hoped for. Lisa had really wanted to avoid drugs, but when twenty hours had gone by and labor hadn't started, they had to hook her up to an IV of a drug called Pitocin.

We walked up and down the halls for hours, Lisa pushing her IV thing, while I ate these vanilla puddings I found in the fridge. Twelve of them I had, and they never appeared on the bill. To me, that's the miracle of birth right there.

Finally, labor started, and I found out why we had taken Lamaze class—birth is painful. I knew that before, but to watch Lisa actually going through it was very traumatic. The worst thing for me about the ordeal was that I couldn't really identify with her pain. It was some kind of awful cramping, unlike anything I could imagine. It would have been much easier on me if, say, every thirty seconds somebody had snuck in the room and whacked her in the head with a big stick. I probably could have handled that better.

"Breathe, honey, breathe!" I'd yell. "Here comes the stick!"

Lisa was a trouper. She went through the whole thing without any pain medication. The doctors would come in occasionally to check her dilation, until finally she was ready for the actual birth. She lay on her back with our birth-coach and good friend, Shelley, on one side of her, and me on the other. We put our hands under Lisa, and every time she had a contraction she'd take a breath and push, while we squeezed her together like an accordion.

After an extremely exhausting hour, Cooper began his entrance into the world. He started to "crown," which is a nice way of saying that the ugly, blue-veined top of his head began to show.

The next thing that happened was like a scene from *Alien*—suddenly his head just popped out! You'd think they'd warn you about that. Five Lamaze classes and they never once said, "Head pops out."

I tried to see who he looked like, hoping nobody, because he was damned ugly at that point.

Then came the actual birth, and I found myself standing there looking at my son, a tiny little old man covered with goo. I was so proud. They took this turkey baster and sucked the goo out of his mouth, wrapped him up and put him on Lisa's stomach. Cooper was about thirty seconds old.

"Hey, Coop man, how you doin'?" I cooed.

He reached out and grabbed my little finger and squeezed it so hard. When I looked at his hand, I saw my hand—a little teeny Ricky hand, no wedding ring, but everything else exactly the same. I started to tear up.

I really lost it when they scooted him up on Lisa's chest, and his mouth—the cutest mouth that has ever existed—was groping for her nipple. It's what the word "precious" was invented to describe. I just sat down and started to cry.

It was the exact opposite of what everybody expected: I was the emotional wreck, and Lisa was calmly taking notes like a rocket scientist.

"Fascinating," she said, feeling the placenta and jotting down her impressions.

32

LIFE IS JUST BEGINNING

One of my favorite things to do now is buzz over Cooper like a giant bee as he lies on his back and watches me. His eyes sparkle and he flashes his gummy grin as he waits for me to swoop in and begin nibbling on his chest. When I do, he grabs my hair and pulls what little I have left out of my head. And then he laughs this laugh that tears at my heart.

I love my son so much, yet I had no idea I would. In a way, I was afraid that I wouldn't. My feelings are so strong that, in a way, I don't know myself. I didn't even suspect that I had this capacity within me. Looking back at my life, I understand why I didn't want to have children, but now I think it was crazy to feel that way. I've seen it done wrong; now I get to do it right. Here's an example: I'll tell Cooper I love him every day of his life.

I can't believe how much I've changed since Cooper was born. I've become so sappy. I used to hate the way people would talk to their kids in that disgusting baby language: "Wook at the wittle poopoo-peepee man." They made me sick.

Today I could write the dictionary of "cute." For example, at our house Cooper doesn't go to sleep— "Cooper-Pooper goes to seepy-seepers." I make myself sick now.

I also used to look at couples with babies and think their lives were over, that they were dead people paying rent from that point on. I think that's the way a lot of people feel who don't have kids. You cling to this sense of freedom. You say to yourself, "I can go out and buy a slice of pizza at three in the morning." Or, "I can sell all the shit I own and move to Montana. I'm unfettered!"

Somehow that's not the way life works.

I sneak into Cooper's room every night to watch him sleep. (He always sleeps on his belly with his arms out in front of him, like the chalk outline of a dead guy.) I never look at him and think that my life is ending. I never even think that his life is just beginning. I always think the same thing—that *my* life is just beginning.

Who would have guessed that responsibility is a necessary ingredient of happiness? Not me—I spent most of my life avoiding it. And the funny thing is that I can't offer this as advice. It sounds like nonsense until you're ready to live it. If somebody had told me two years ago that a lack of responsibility was keeping me from real happiness, I would have thought they were crazy.

It is very difficult to put certain things into words, because it seems like everything's already been said. There are no new truths to be uncovered—just the old ones to be dusted off from time to time. For example, having a child really does put your life into perspective.

I now believe in free will. I can't prove that it exists, but I feel it does, which is even more important. You can do anything in life you want to do. Ouch! Sounds a little trite, doesn't it? Well, that's what having a baby can do to you.

Imagine walking into an elevator full of people and as the doors close, turning toward them and shouting, "I am king of the elevator!" As hard as that would be to do, you know that you could do it—it is within your power. You can walk over to your television set right now and smash the picture tube. You can stop smoking. You can lose weight. All you have to do is think you can.

Say you want desperately to write a book but don't have the discipline to do so. Just sit down tonight and write one page; that's not that hard. Tomorrow write another page, the next day another. In a year you will have a 365-page novel. A shitty novel, yes—but a novel nonetheless.

I'm also beginning to see that this thing I've feared for so long—my own death—is an absolutely essential ingredient of my life. I have to die. Not just to make way for Cooper's generation, though that is part of it. It's so much more than that. My death gives the time I spend here some meaning. It gives scope and definition to my life. In much the same way that love must have the power to hurt in order to feel so wonderful, we would never know anything of happiness if we weren't aware of our own mortality. Death is the counterweight of all that is good.

It seems clear to me now that time is precious only because it's limited. What if nobody ever died? Think about it. There'd be an awful lot of people who could ride the bus for a quarter.

I used to have a fear that watching my child grow older would make me feel older myself. What I didn't understand at the time is that everybody is amazed that they are as old as they are—that everybody feels younger than their actual years. I didn't realize that time past—the memories and experiences of a lifetime—is just as valuable as time ahead—the potential of youth. And I certainly never realized that neither of these is as important as time present—living in the moment.

Don't get me wrong though. I'm not saying I don't still fear death. Of course I do. Hey, I fear life. I'm pretty sure that's why God and humor were invented in the first place.

For my mother,
whom I have never stopped loving.